Just like Roodie

Yelitza Smith

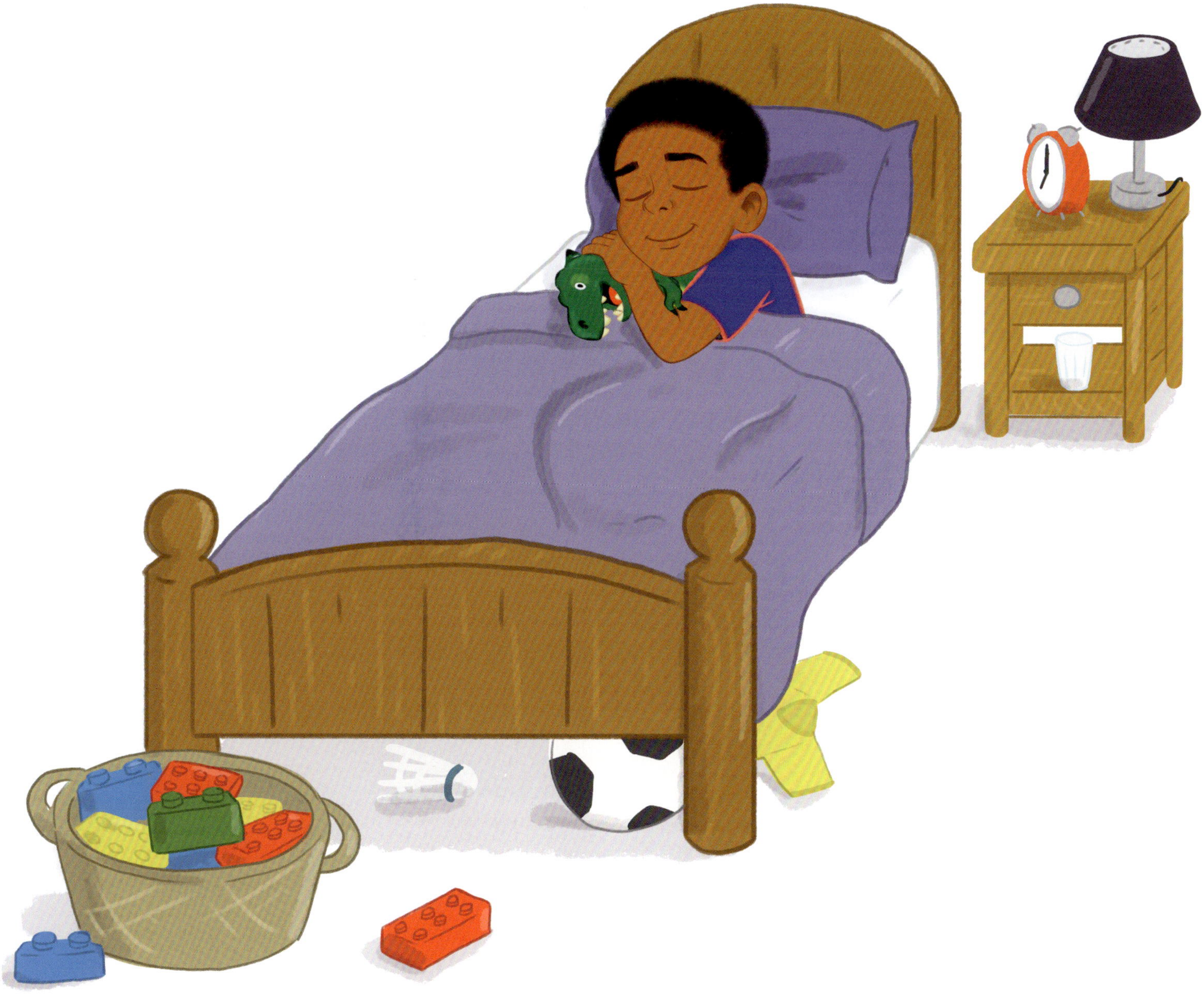

Collins

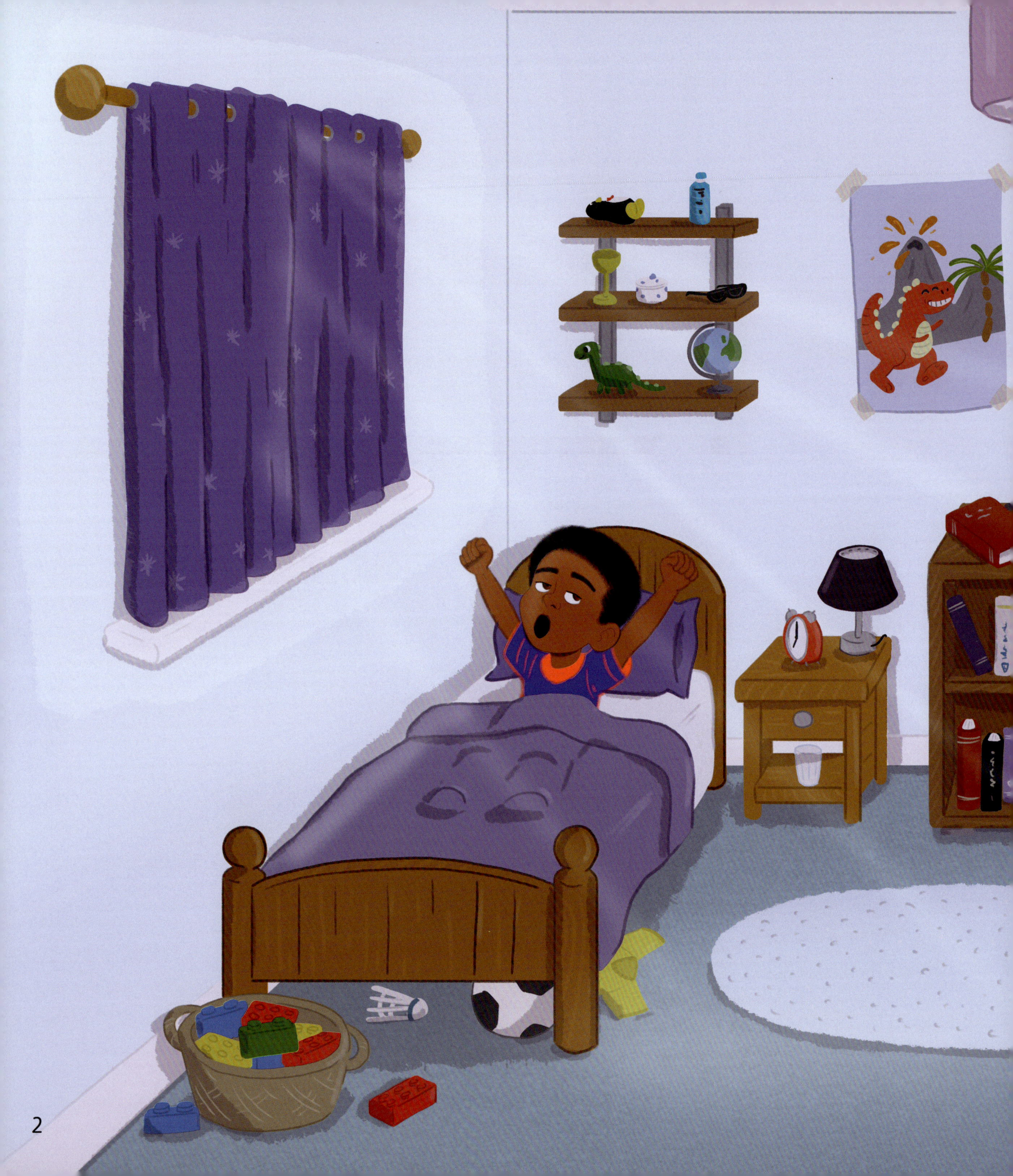

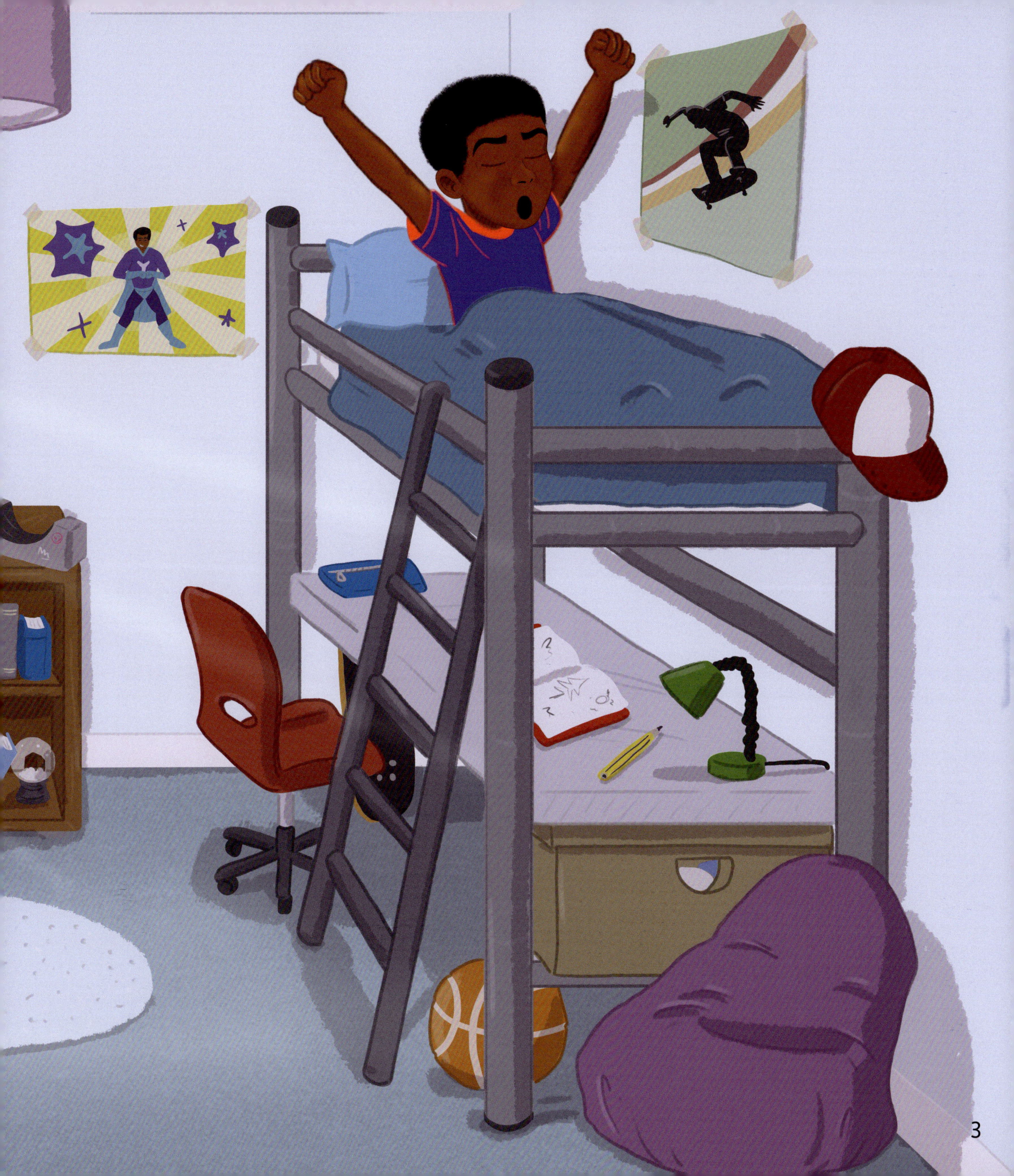

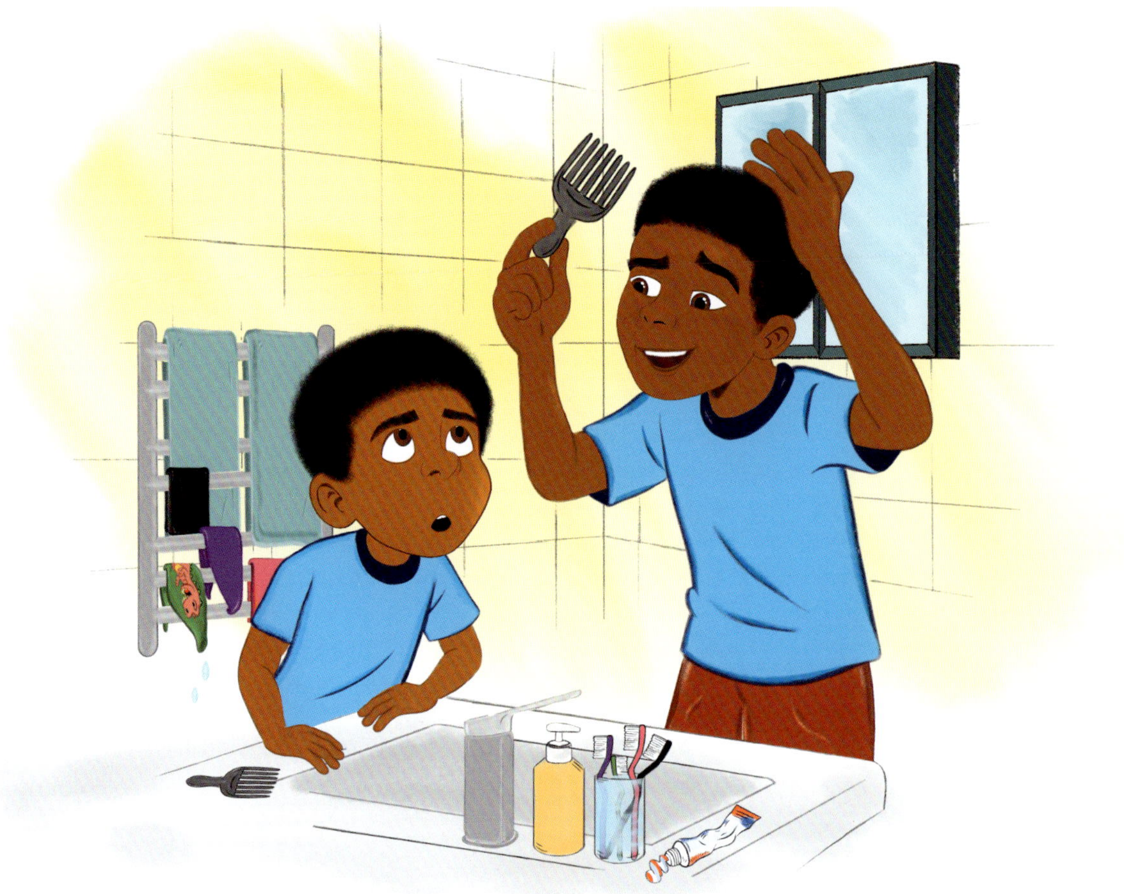

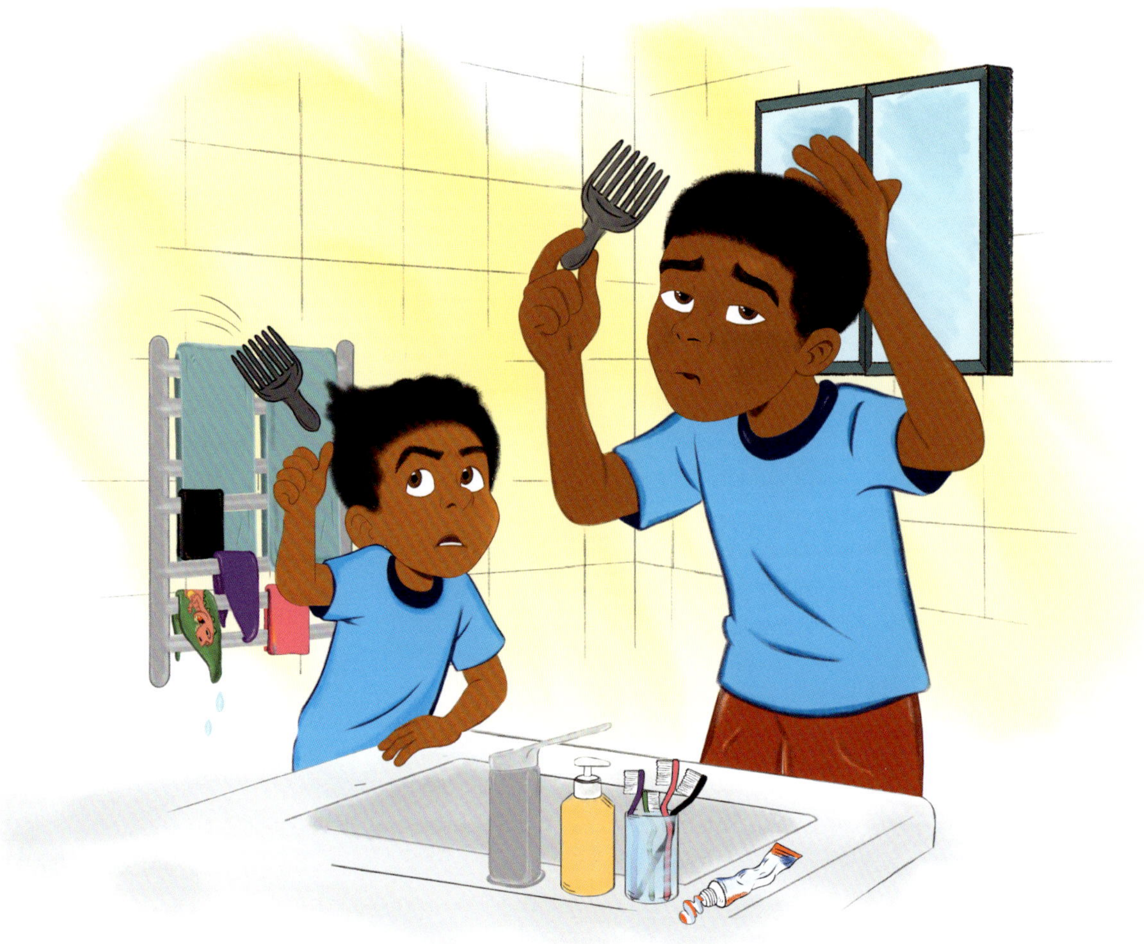

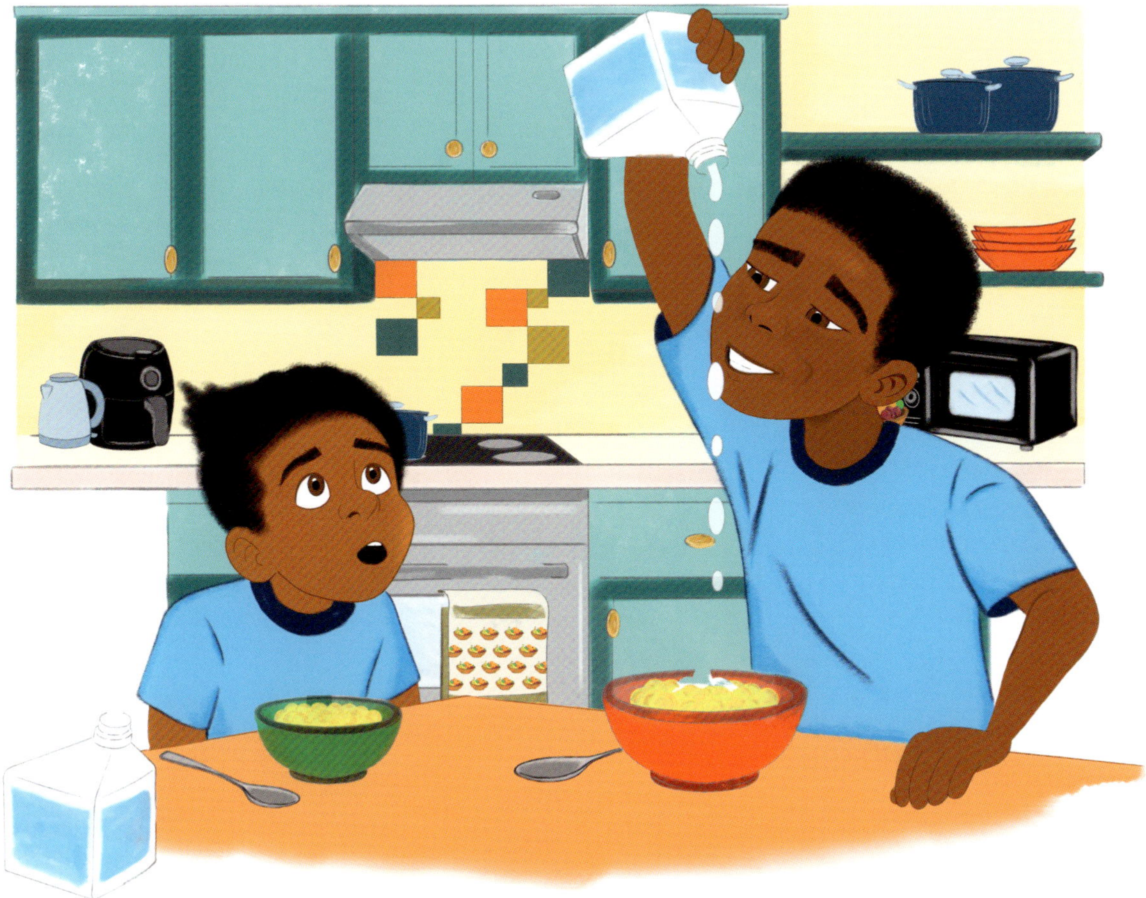

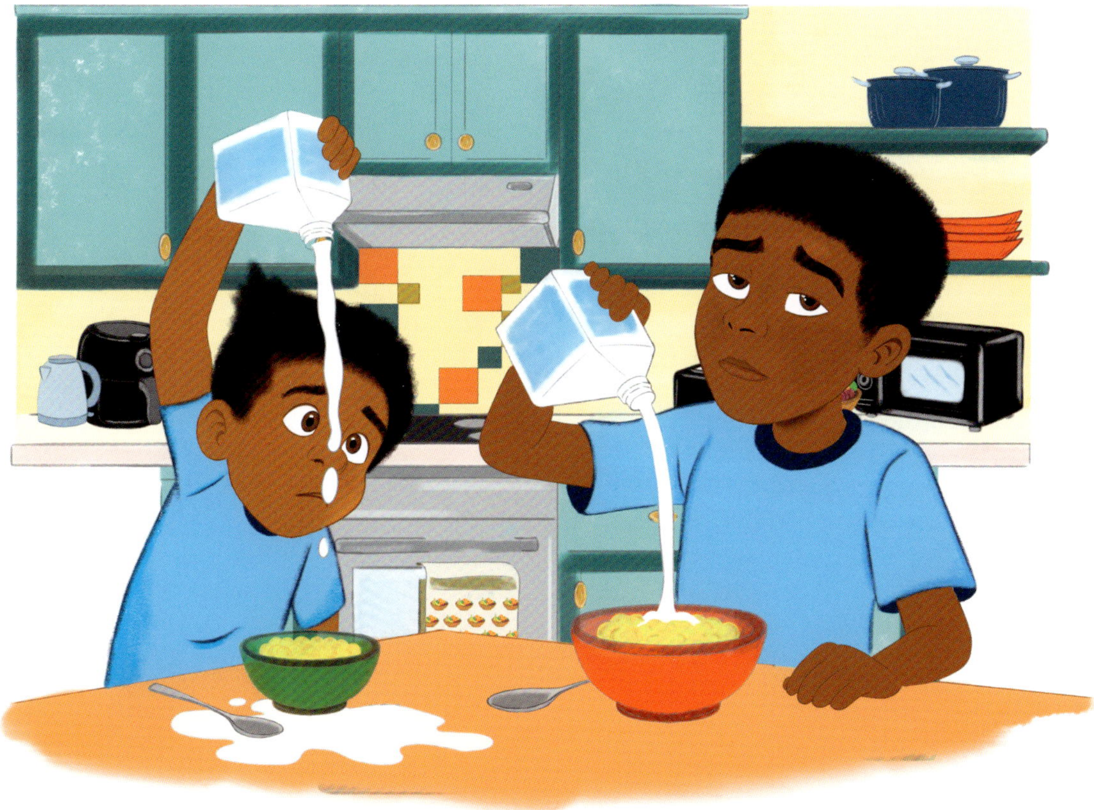

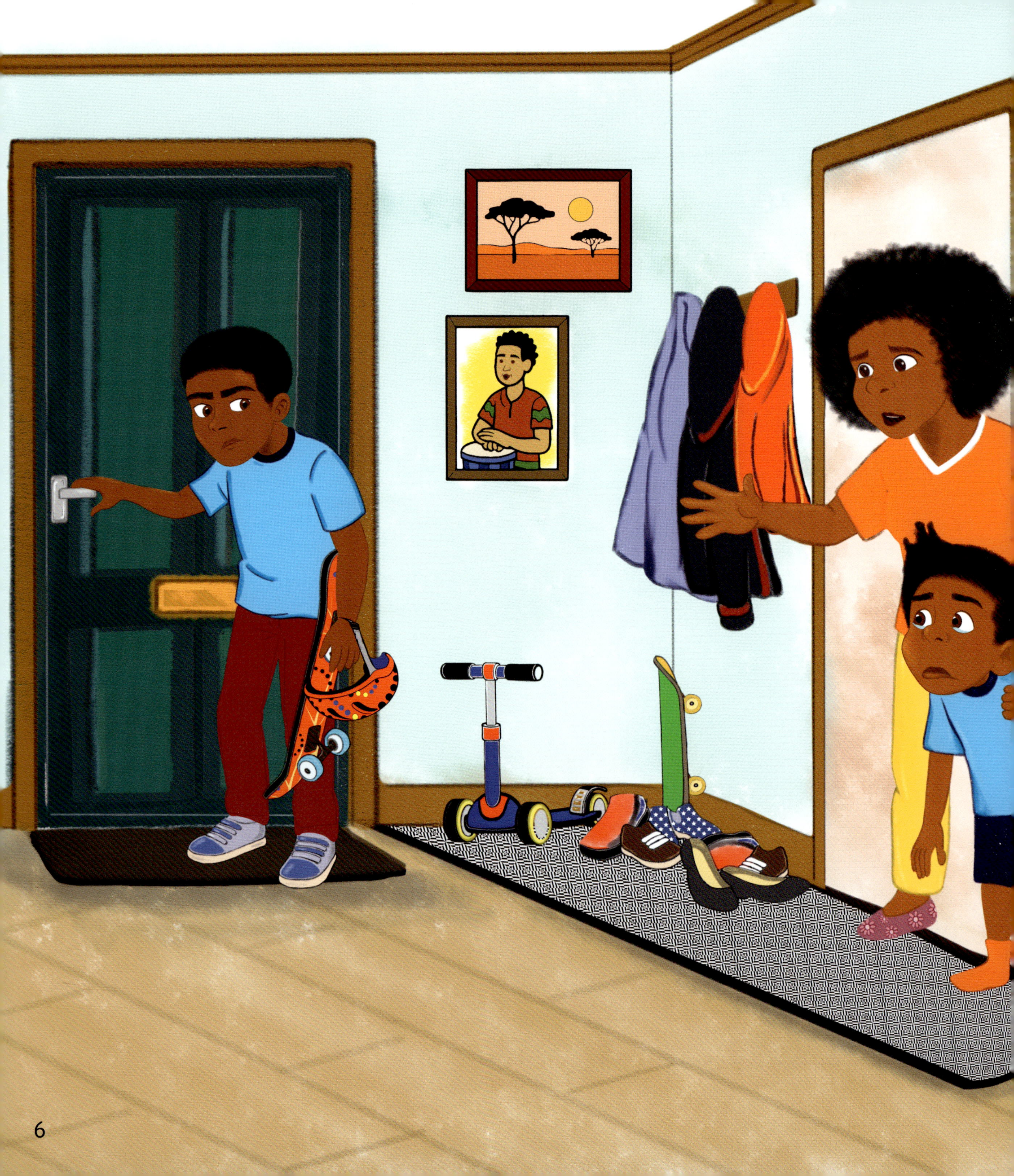

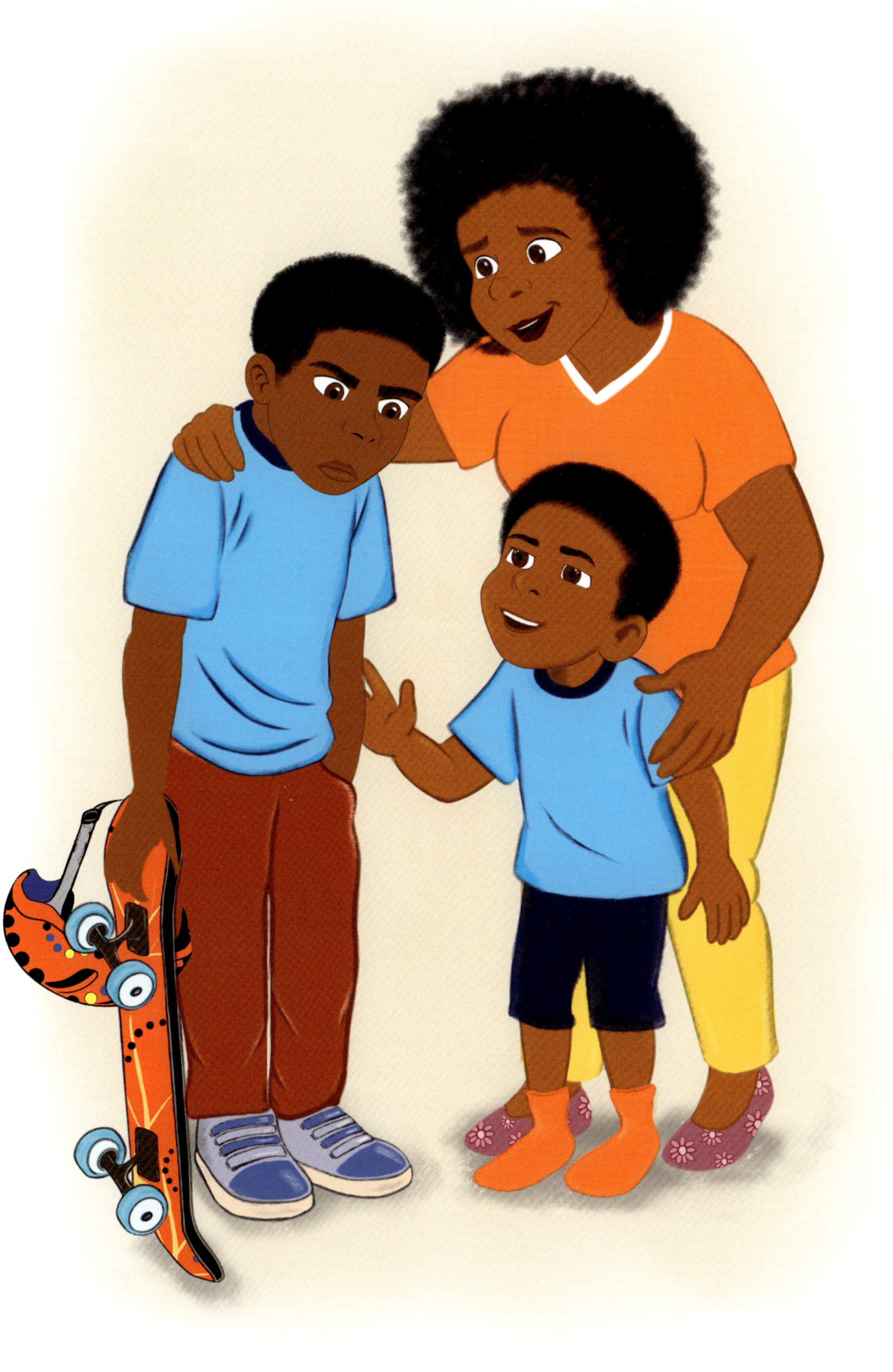

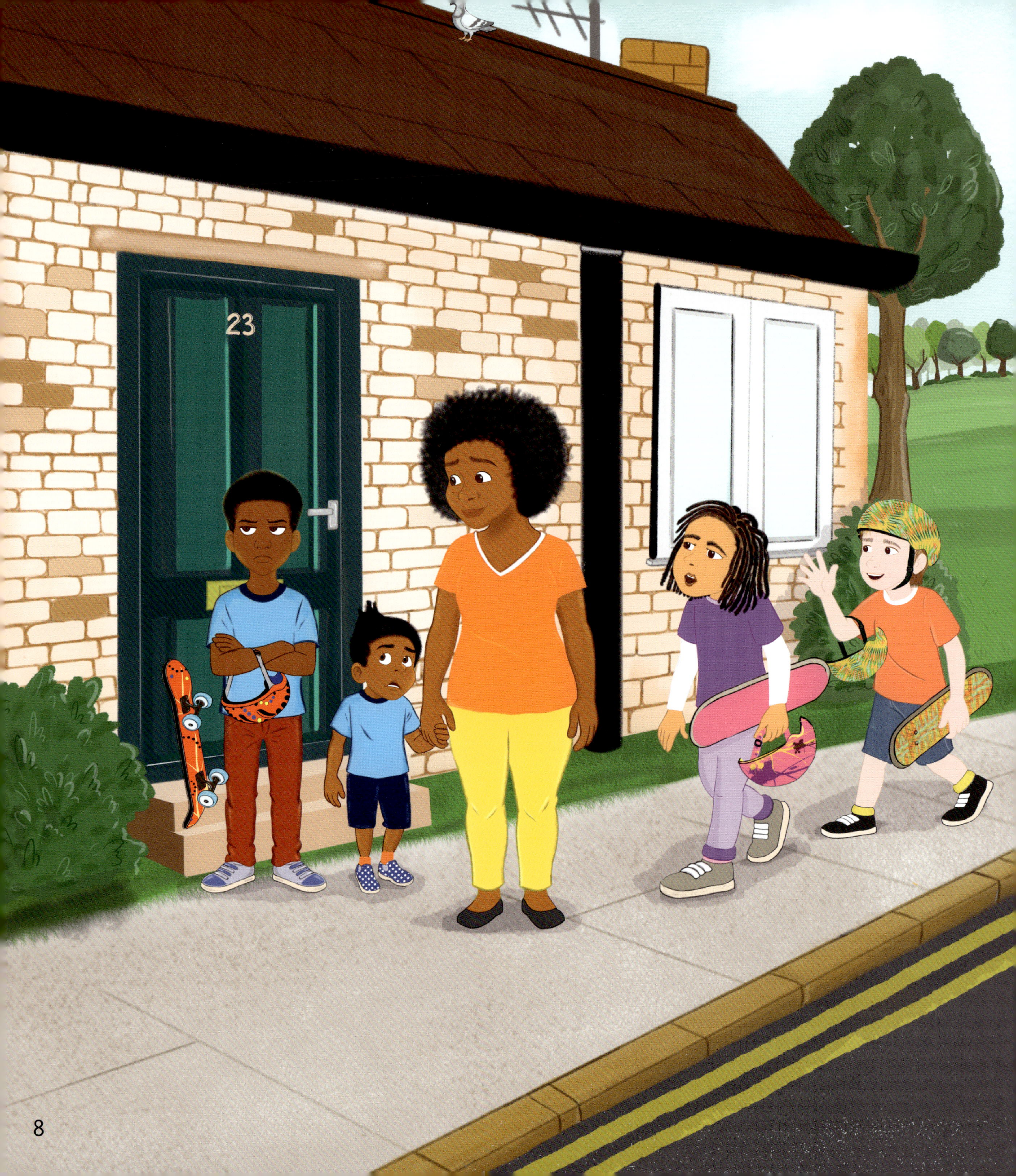
23

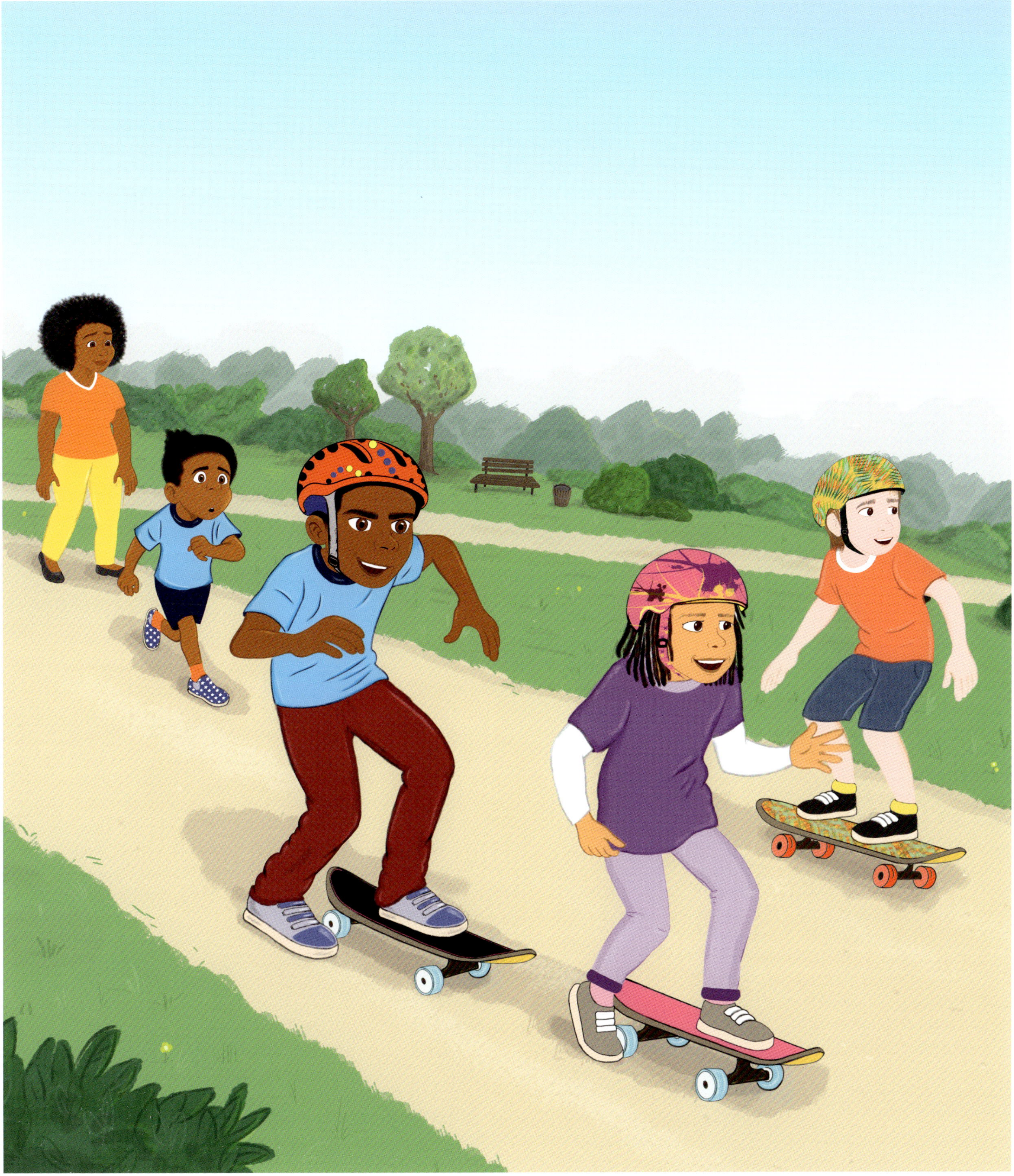

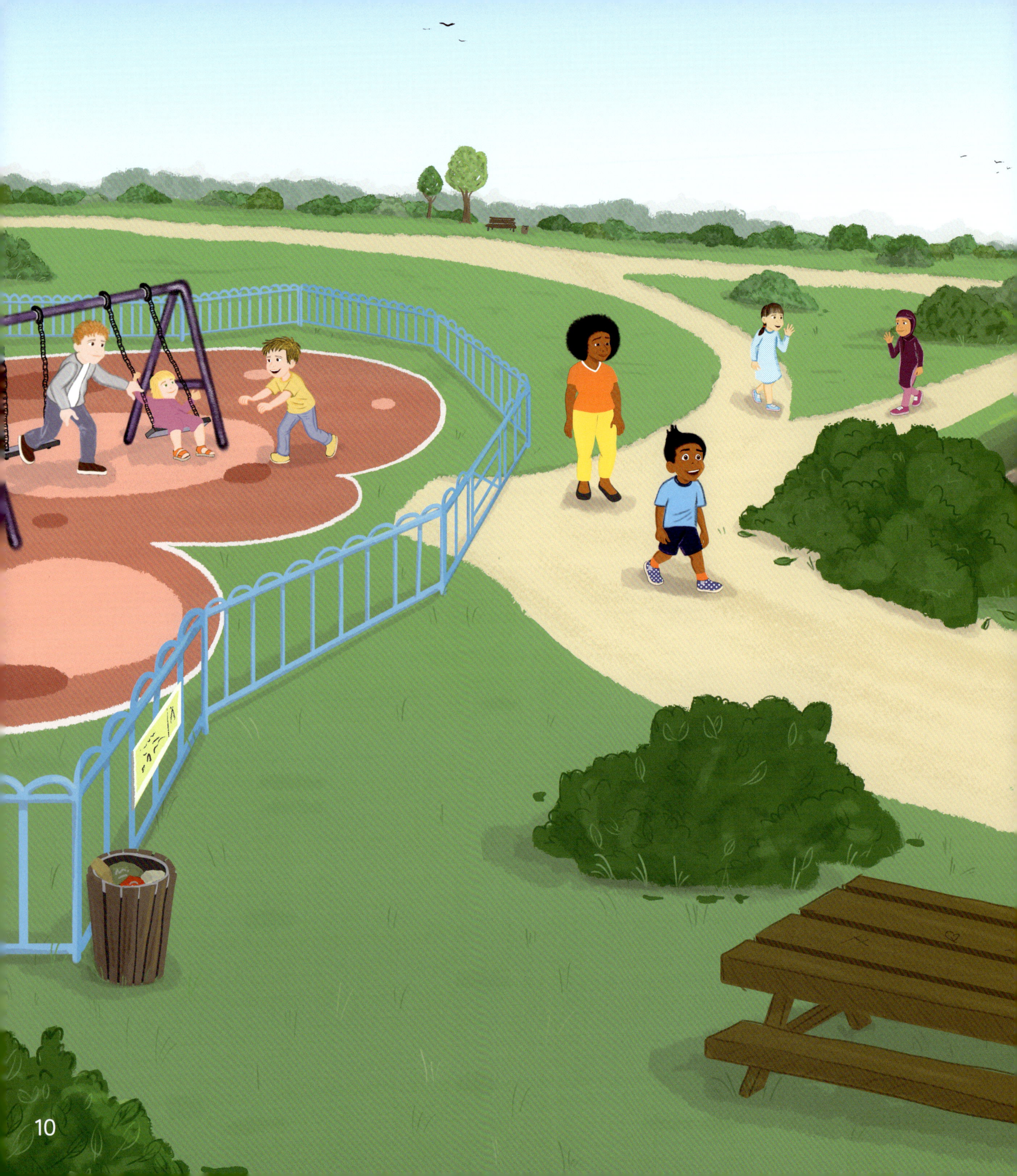

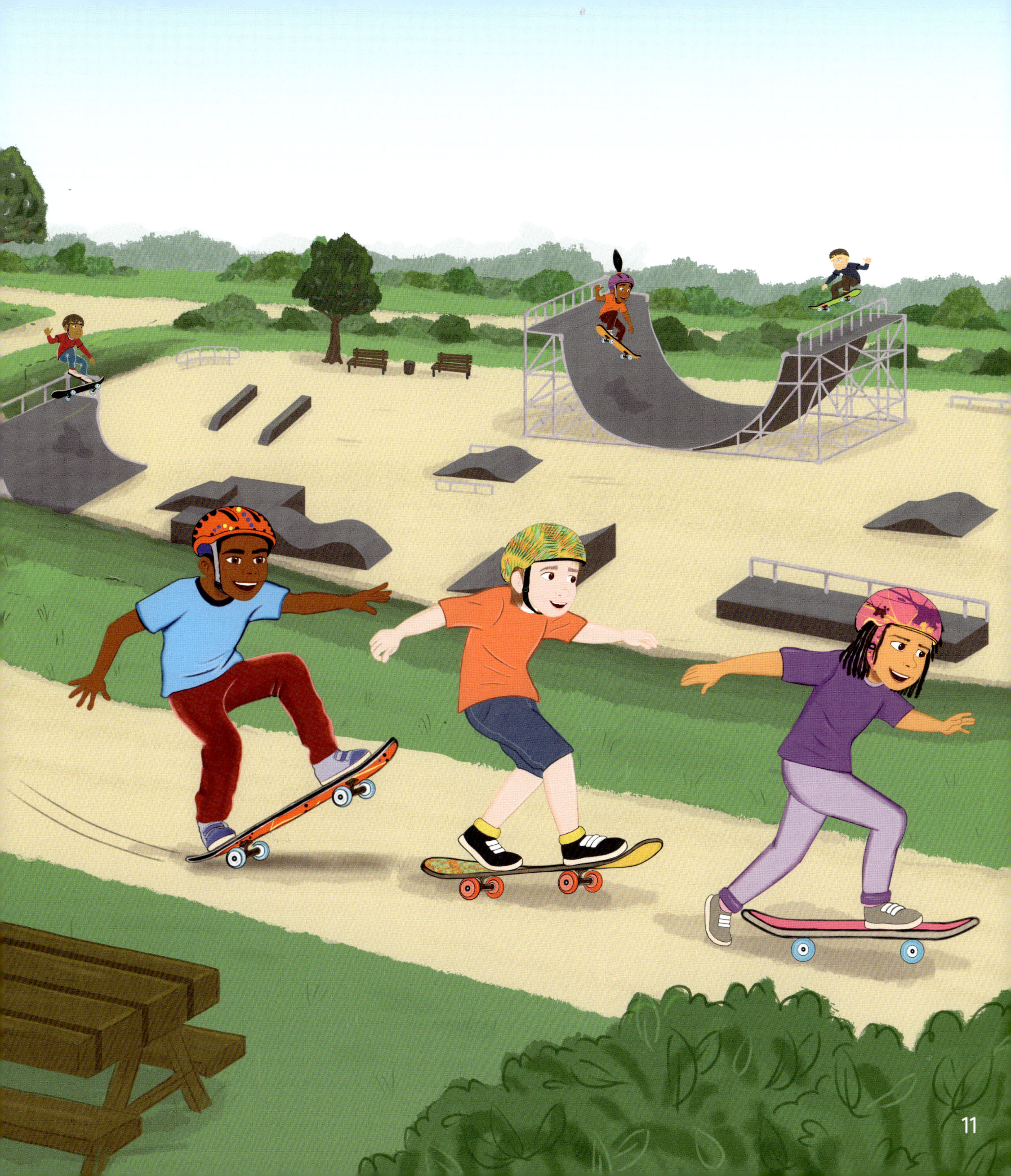

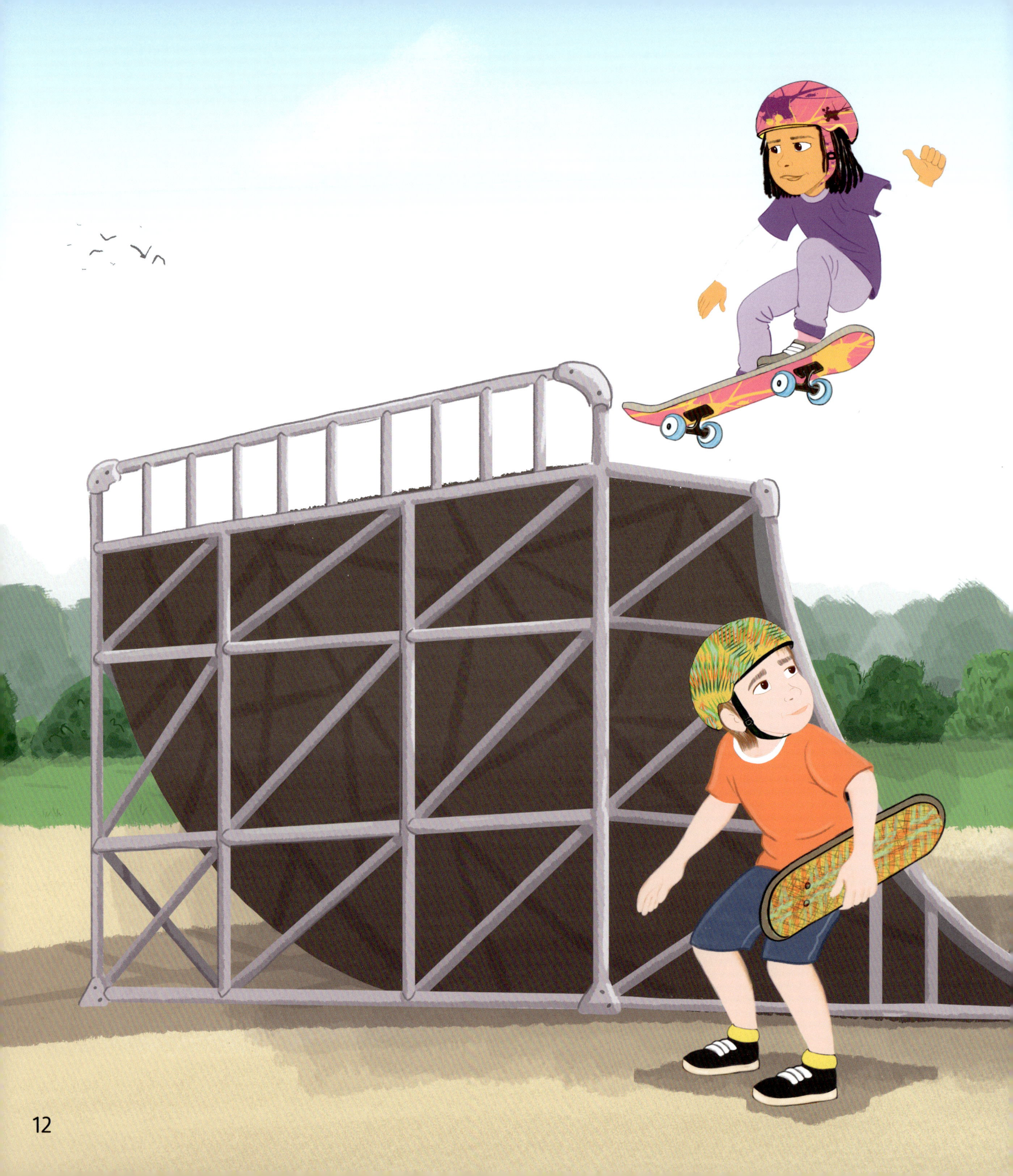

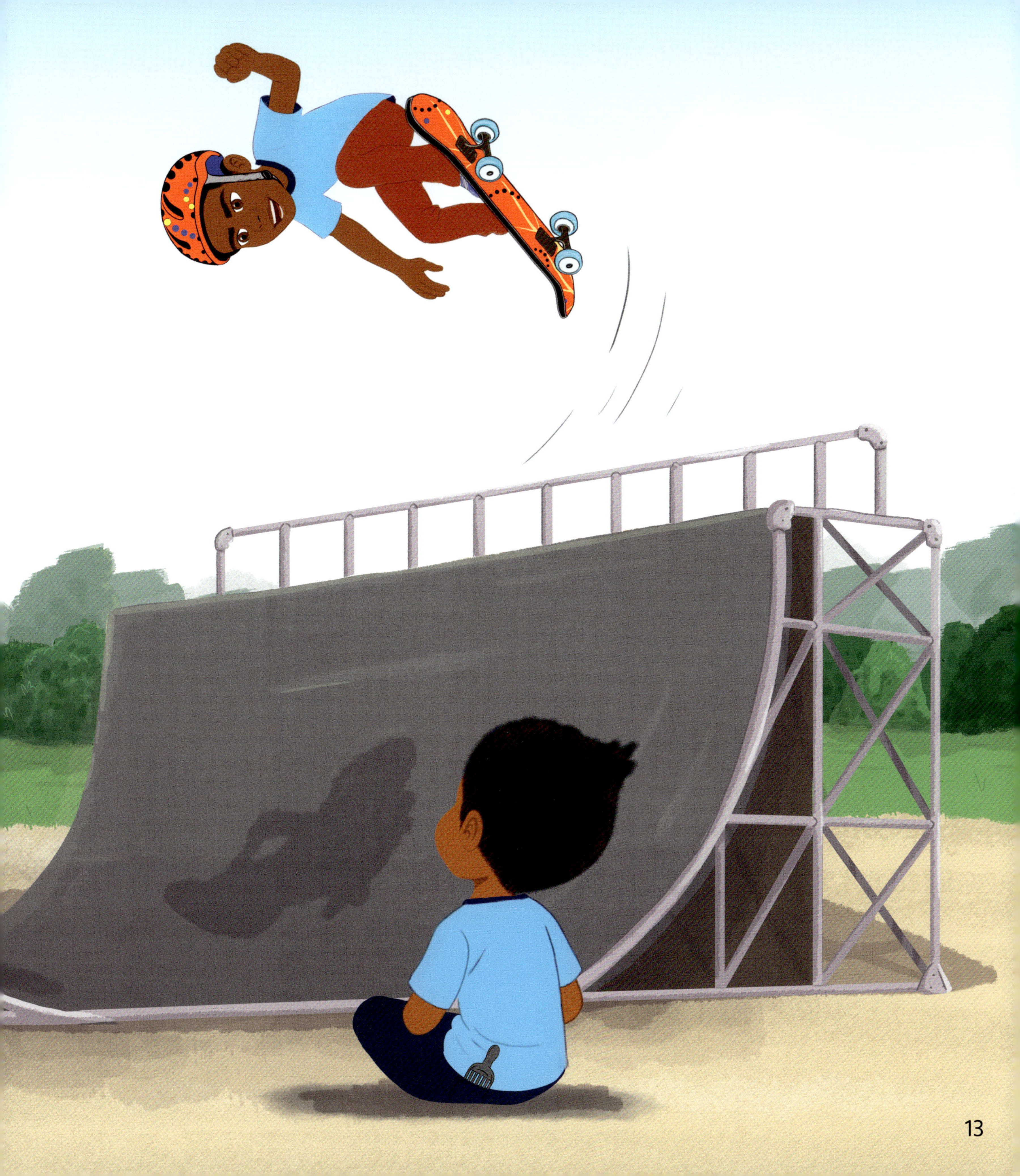

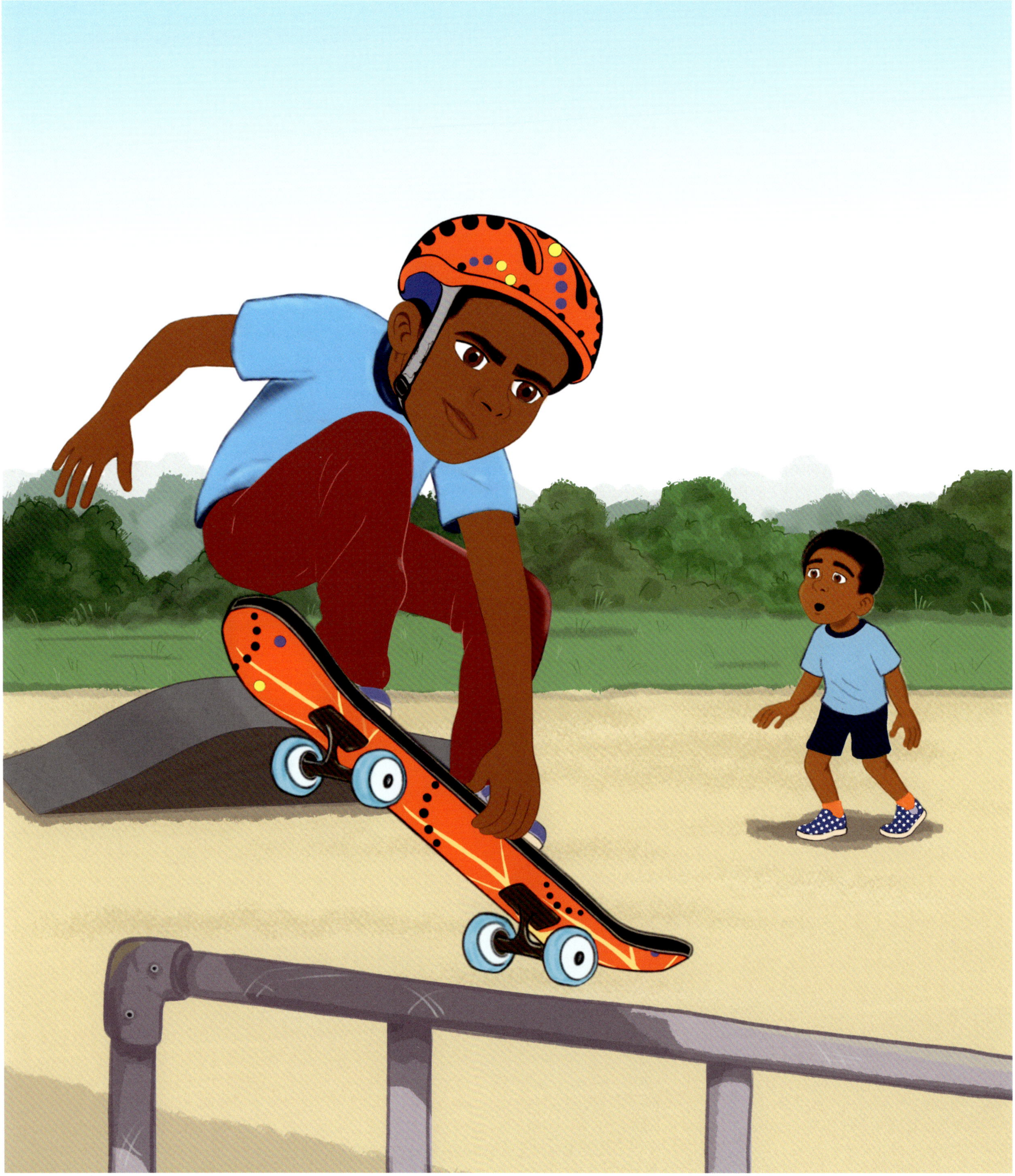

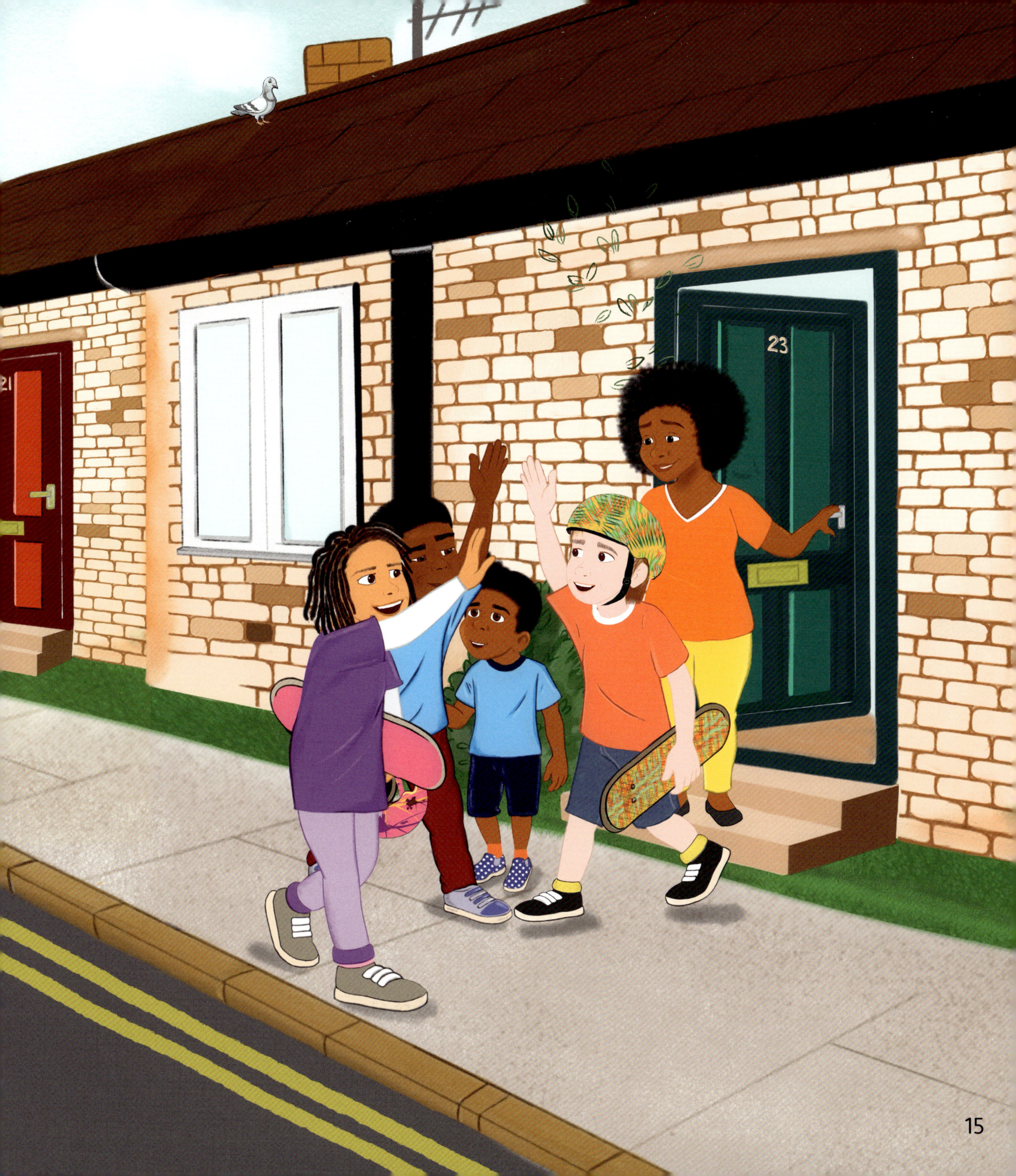
21
23

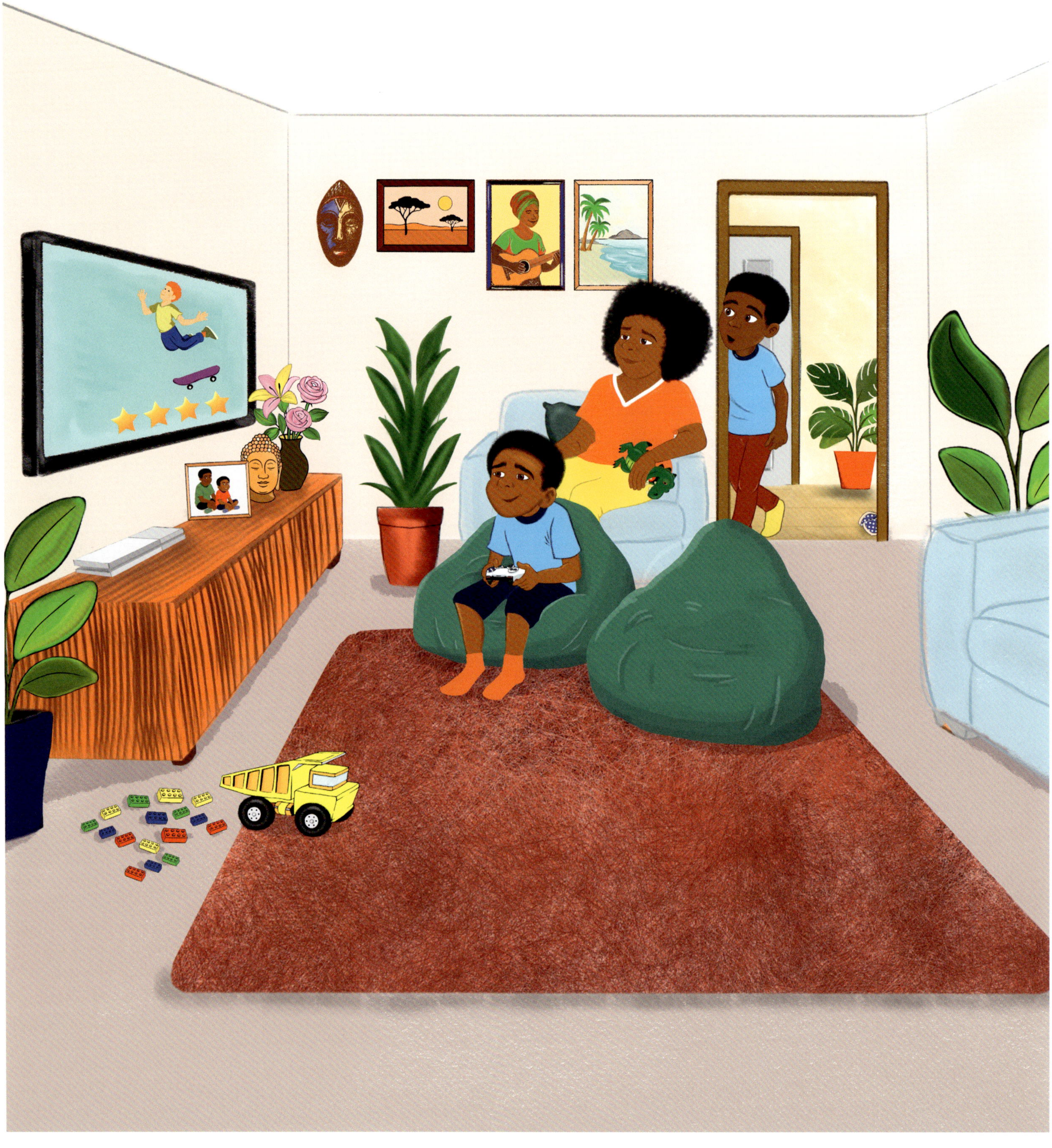

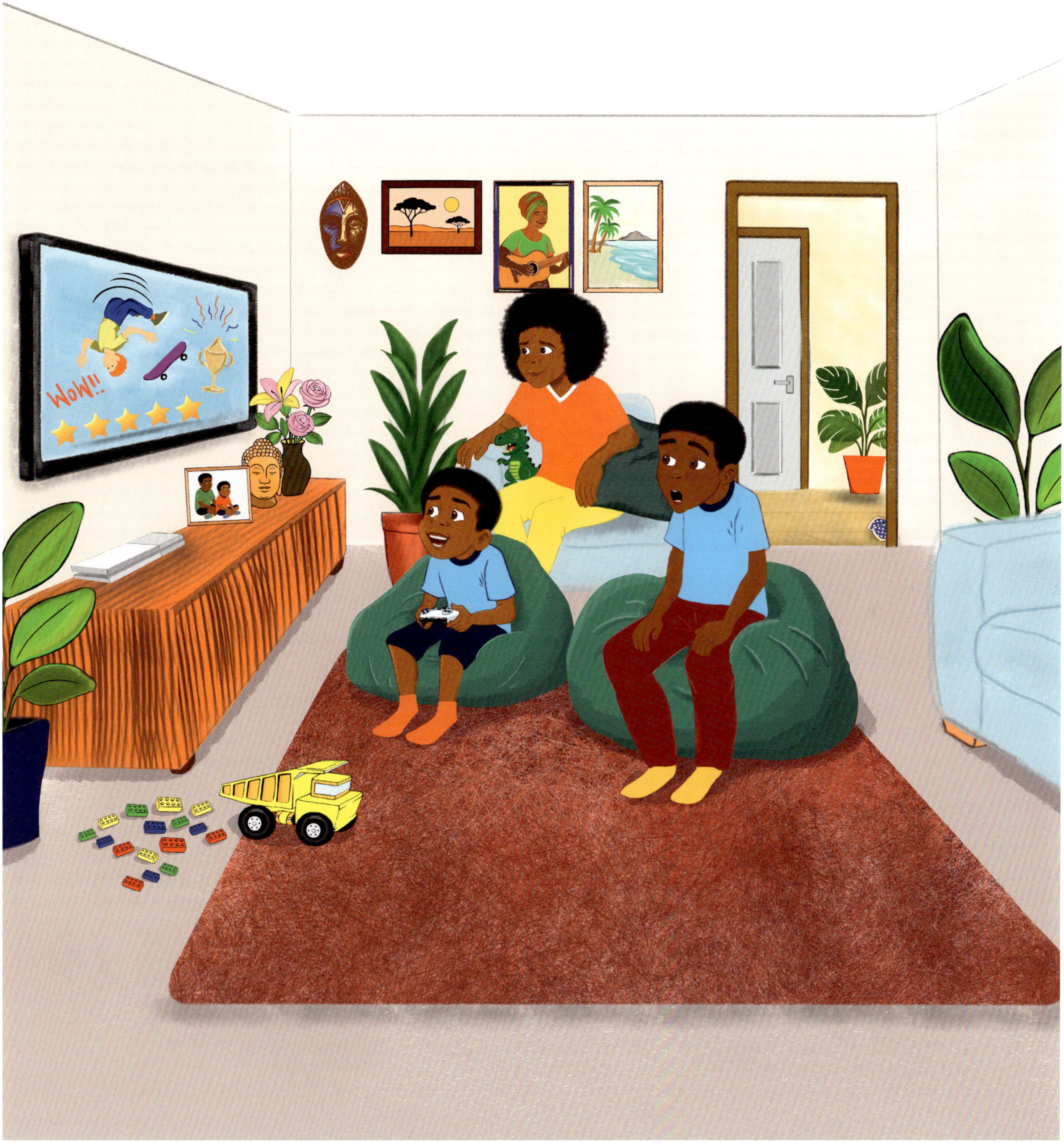
WOW!!

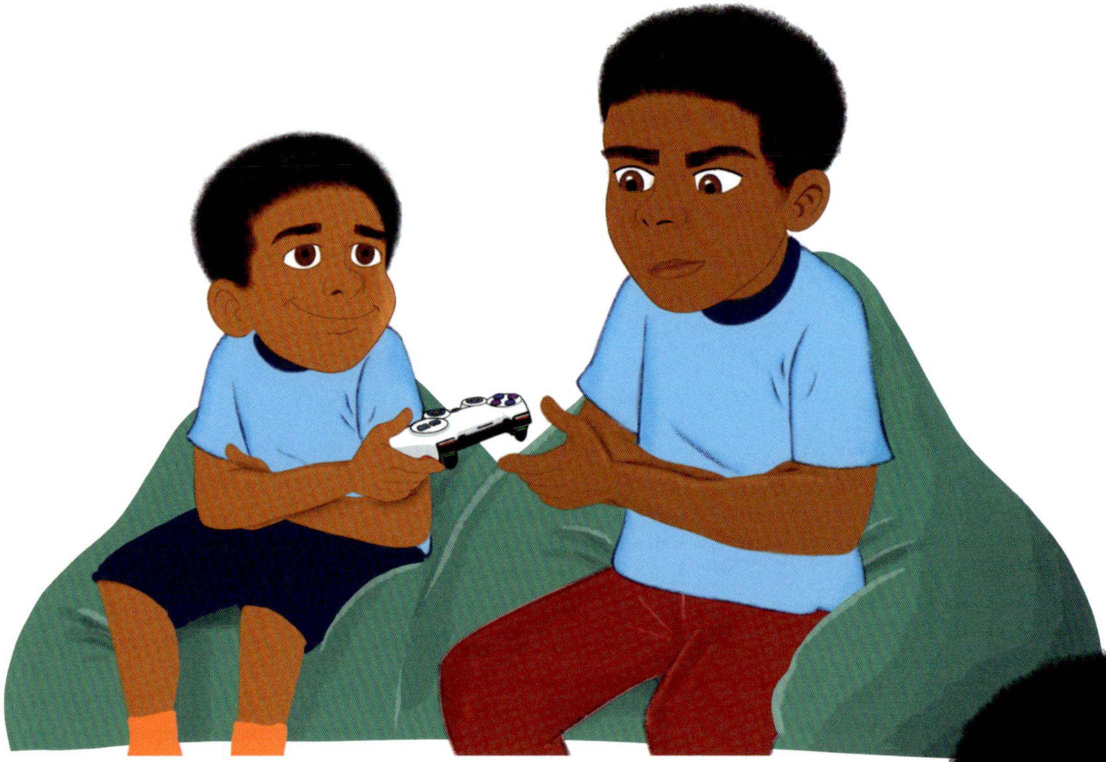

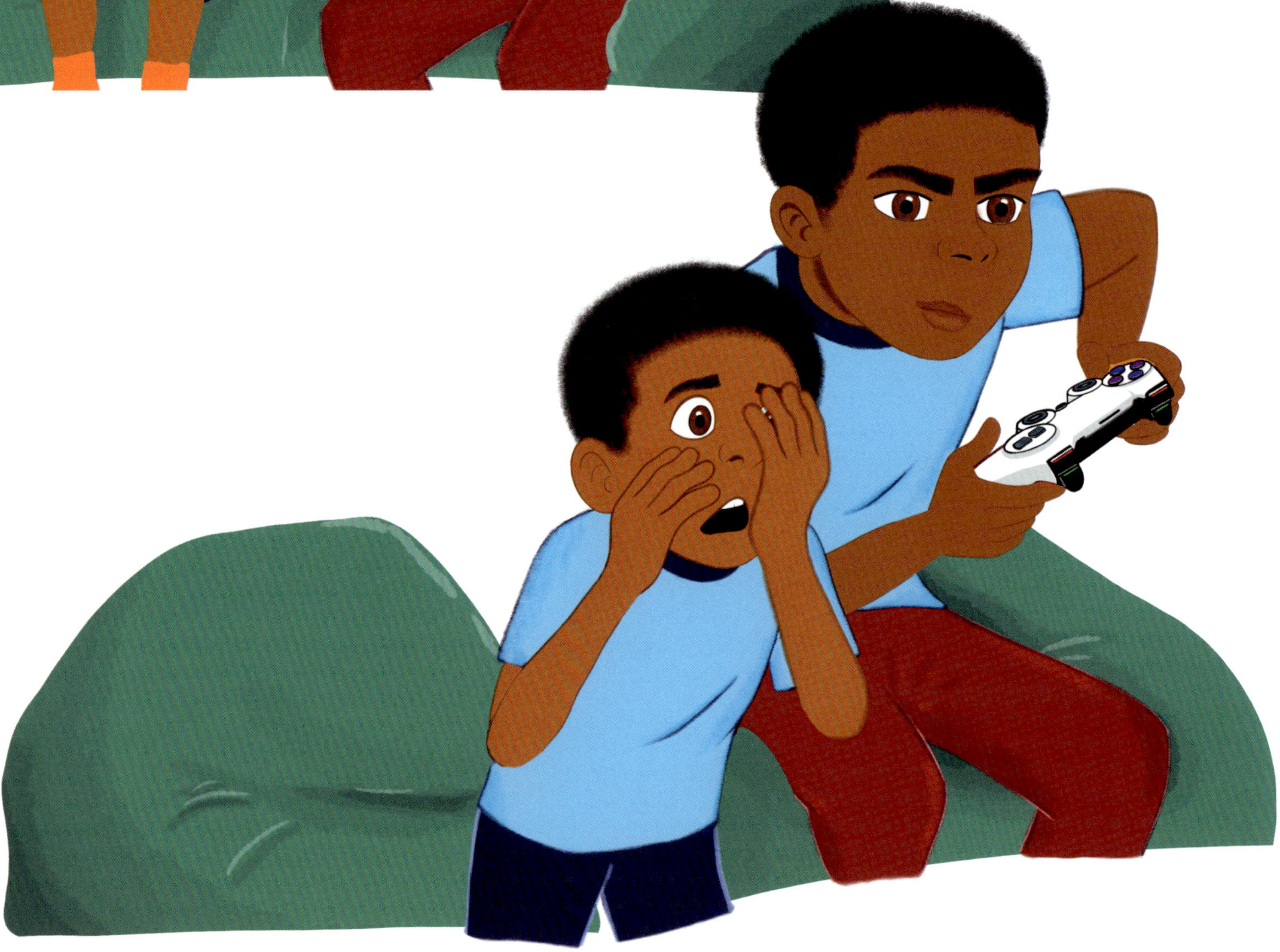

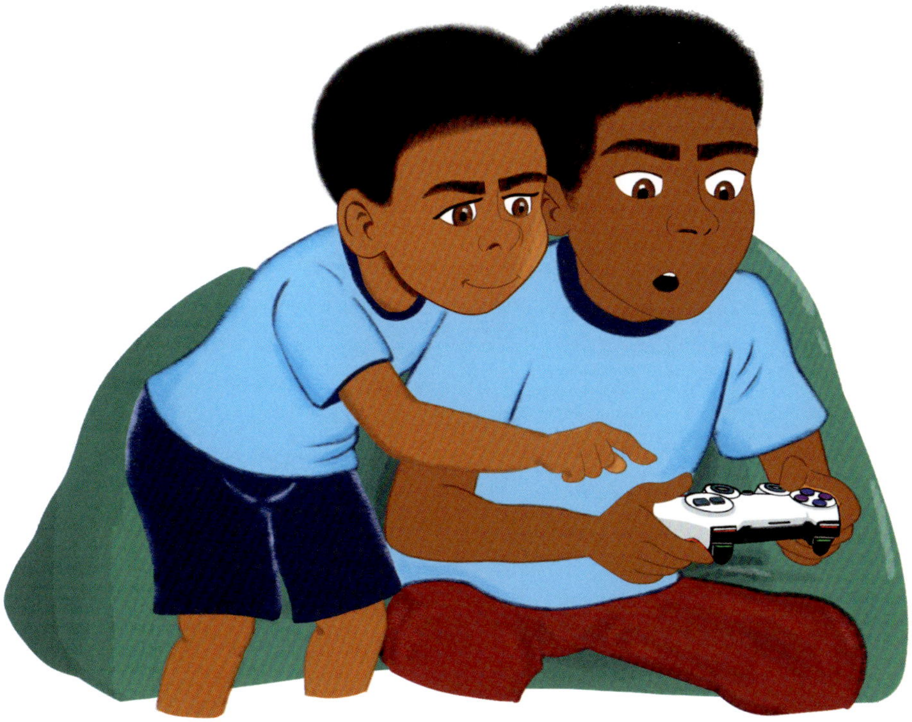

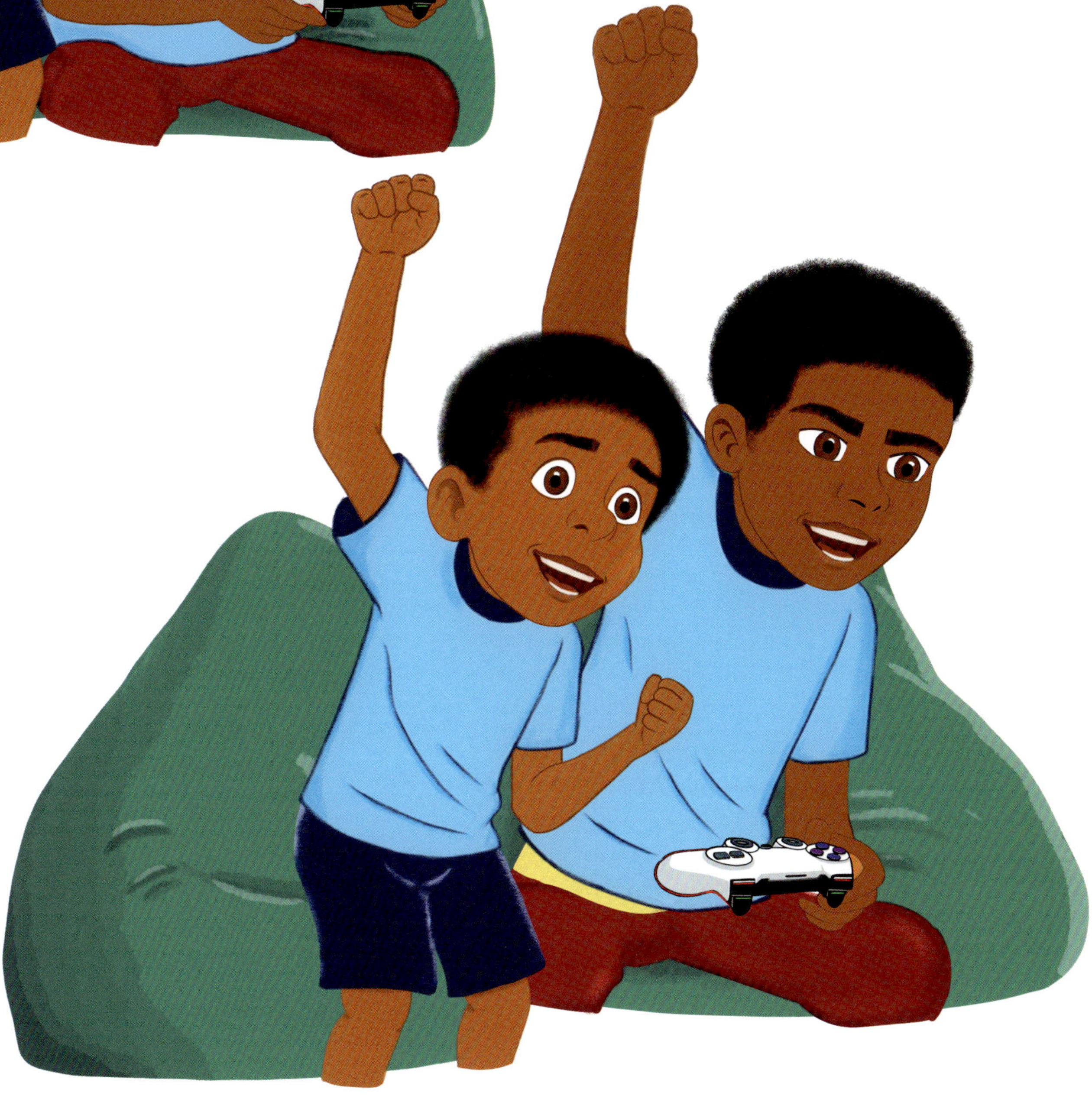

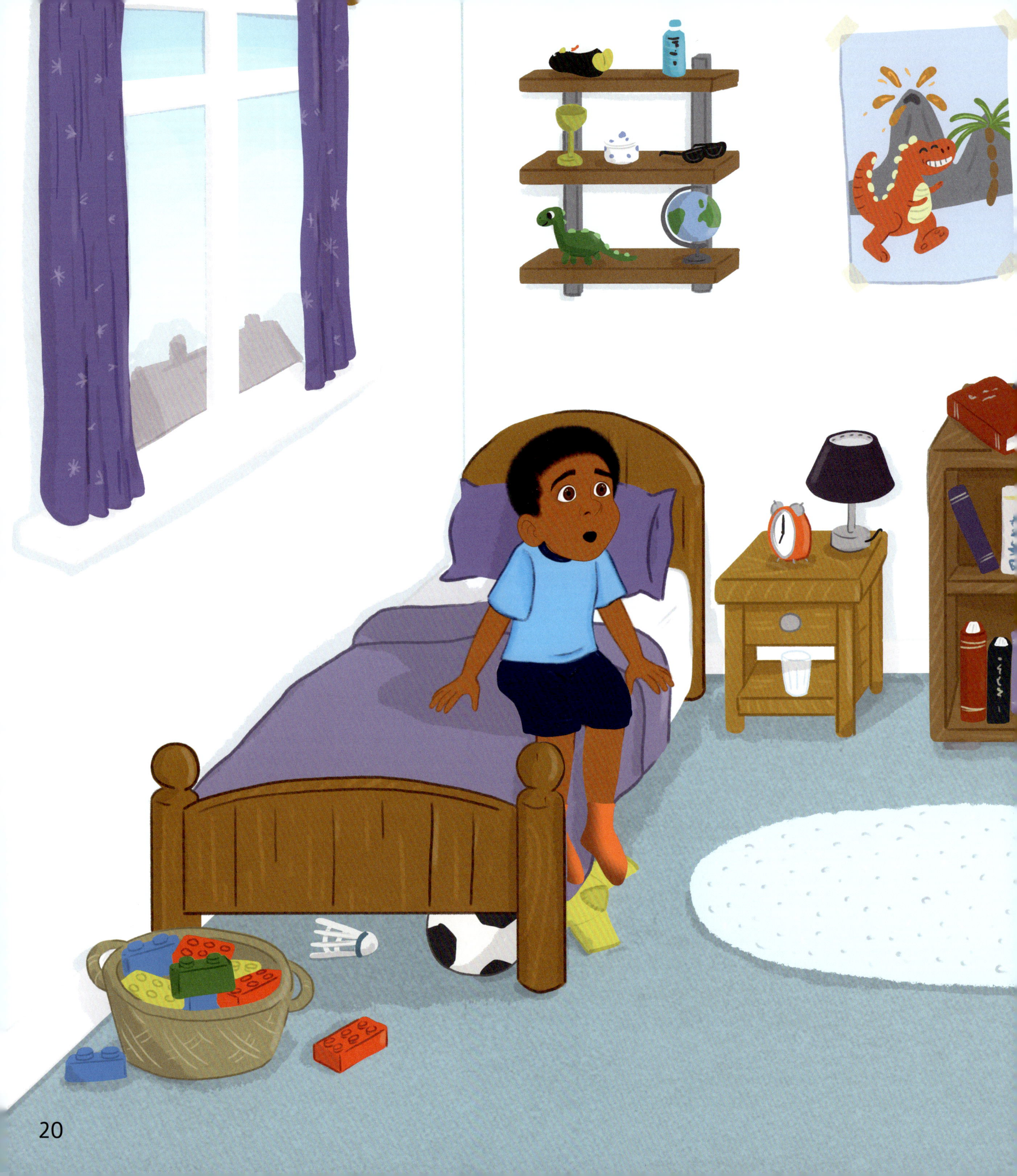

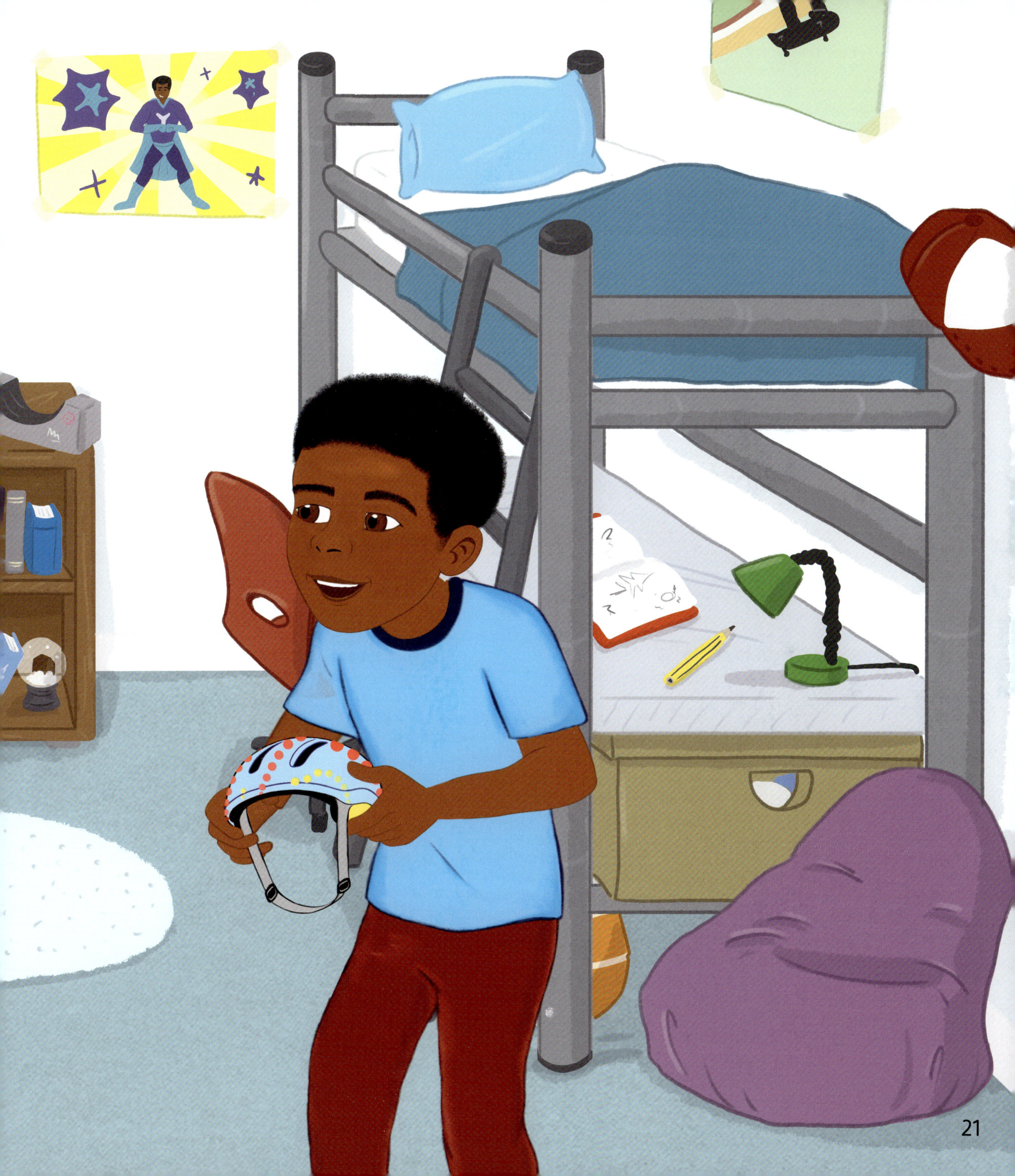

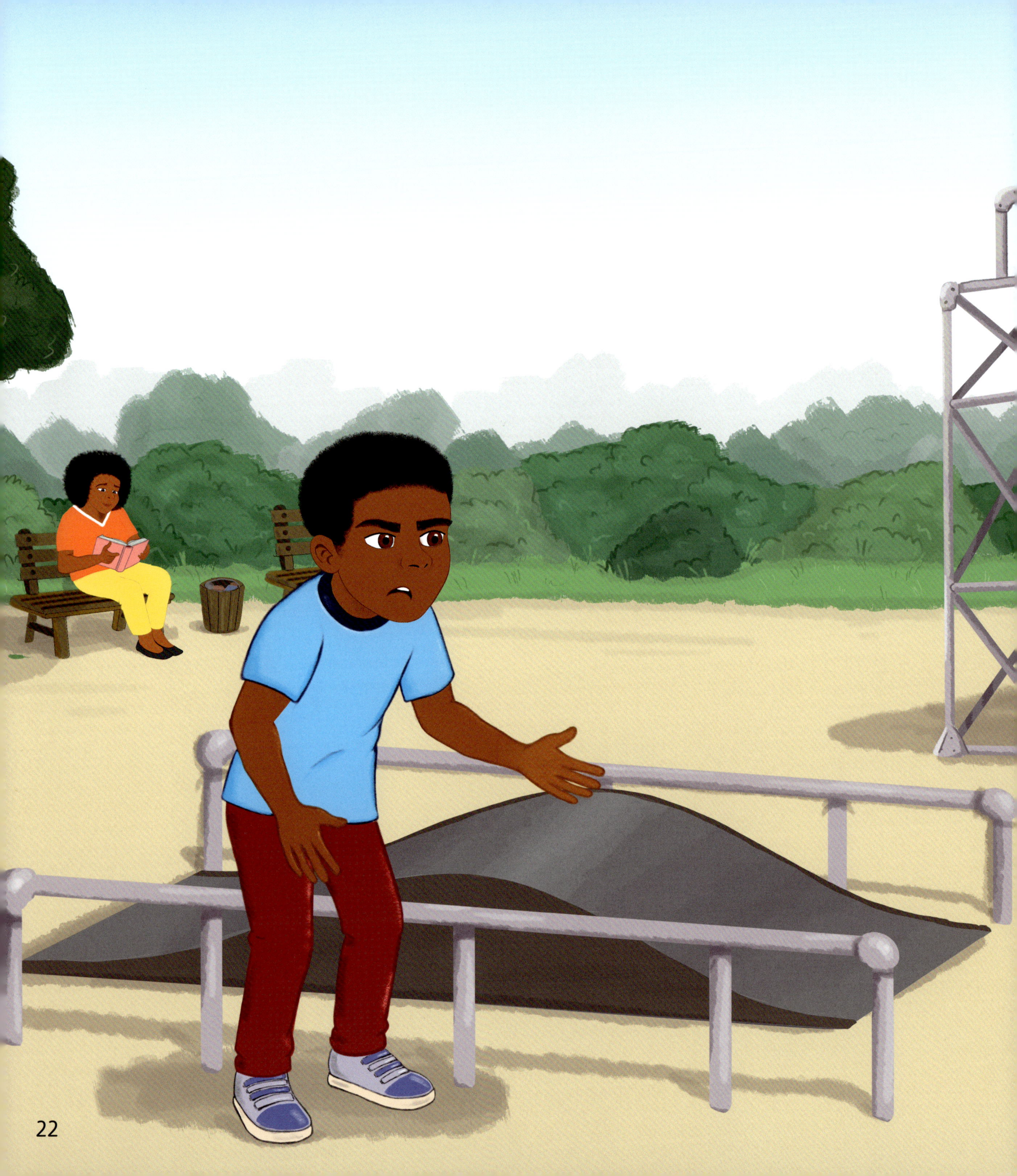

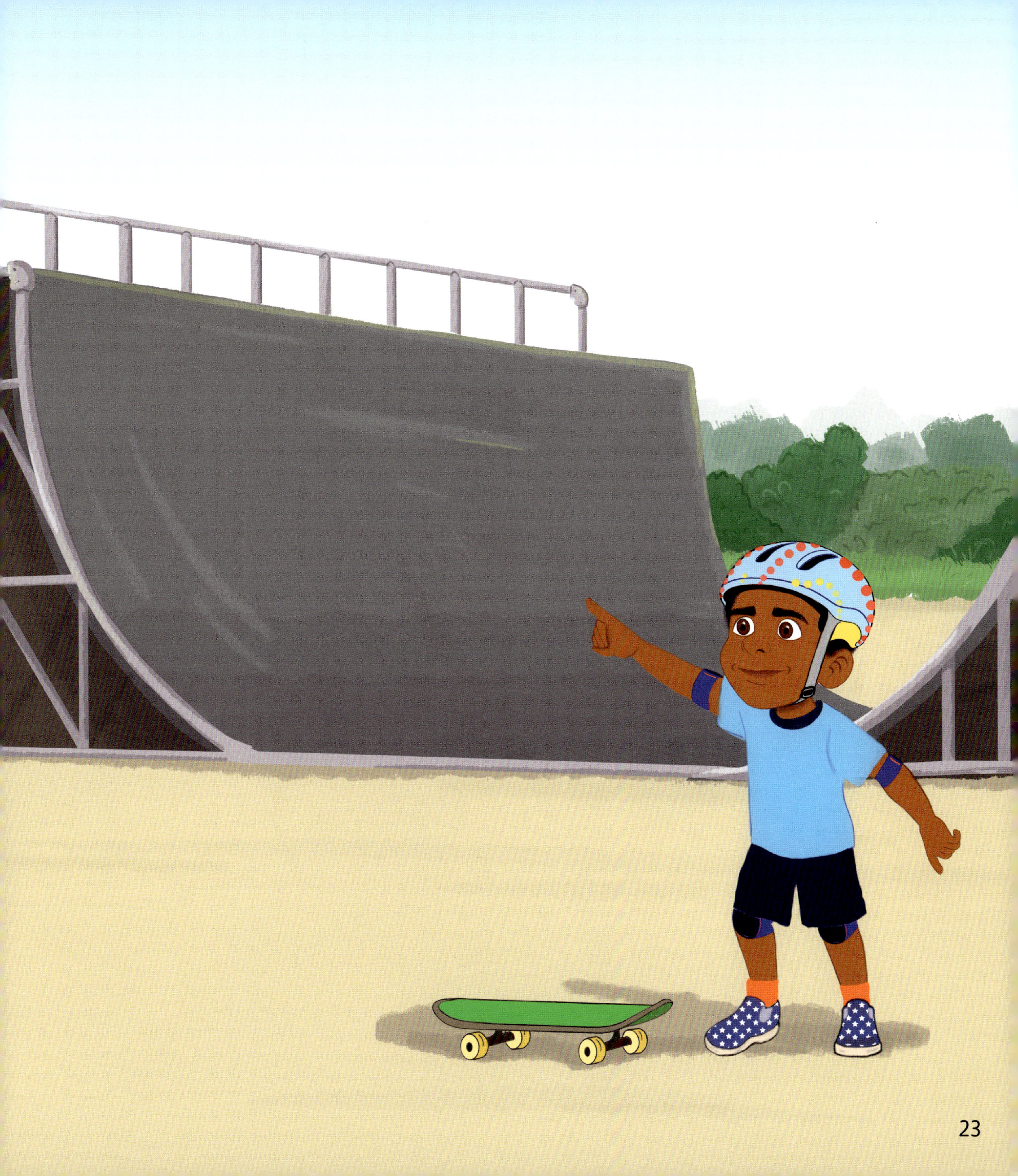

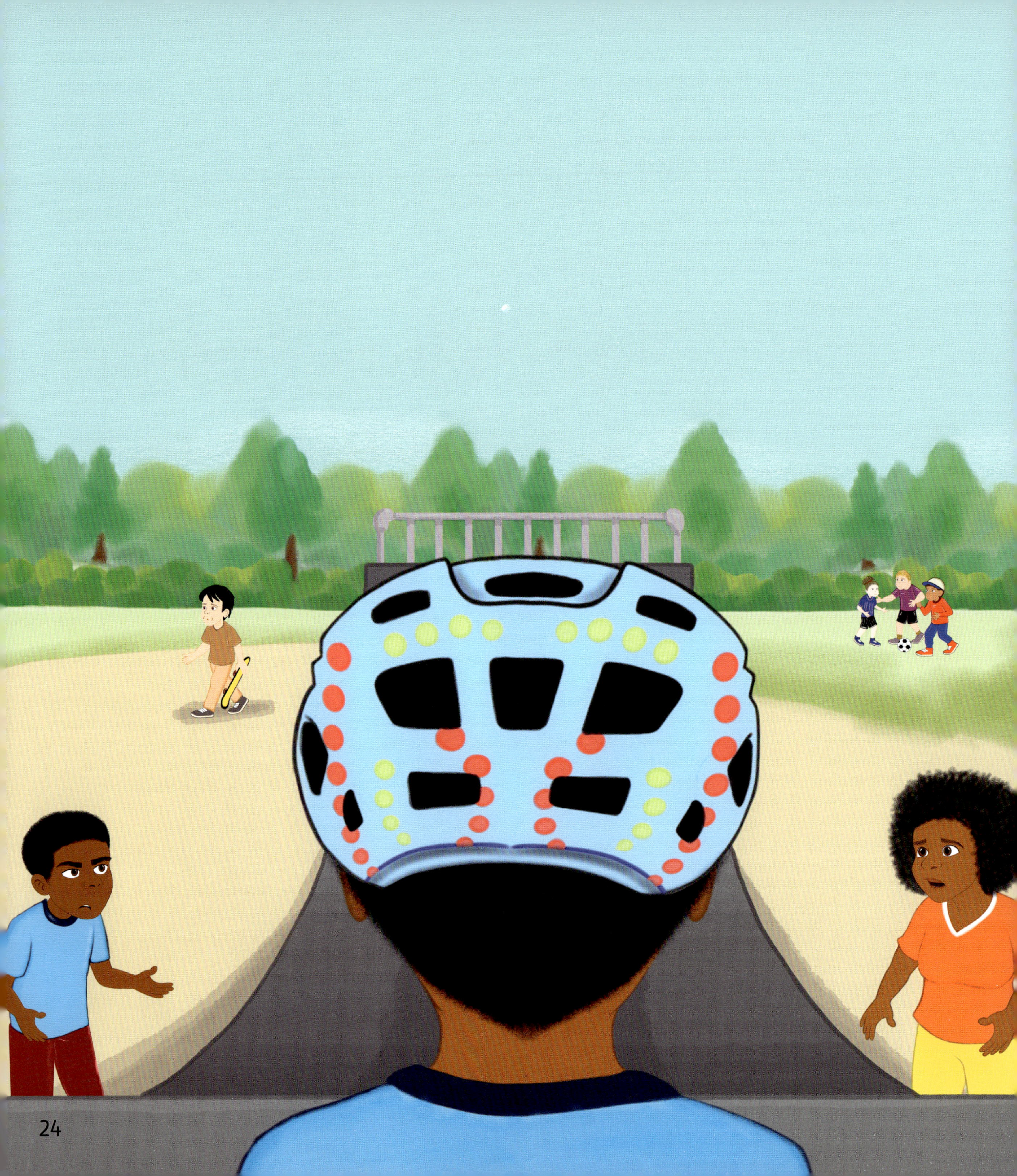

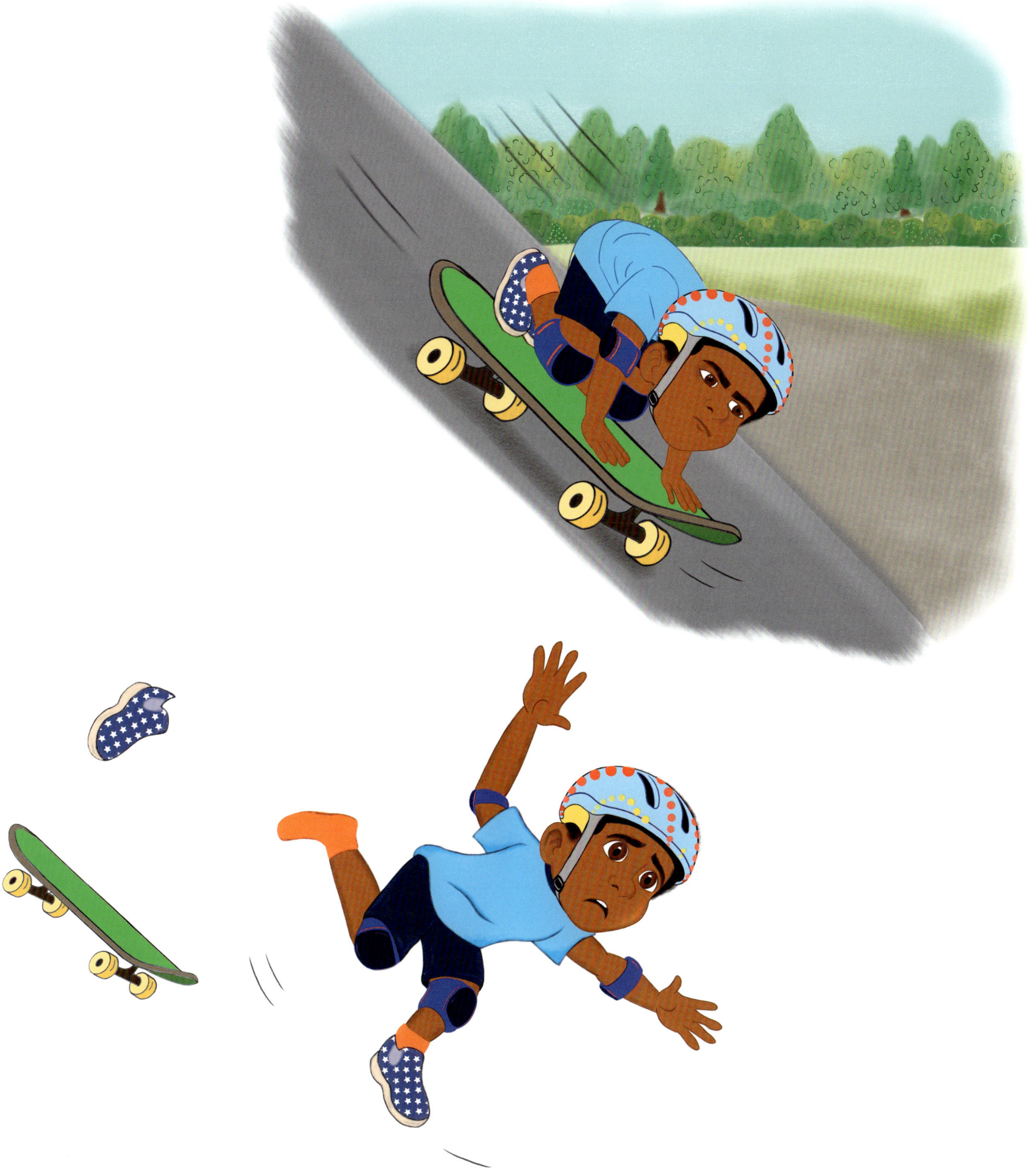

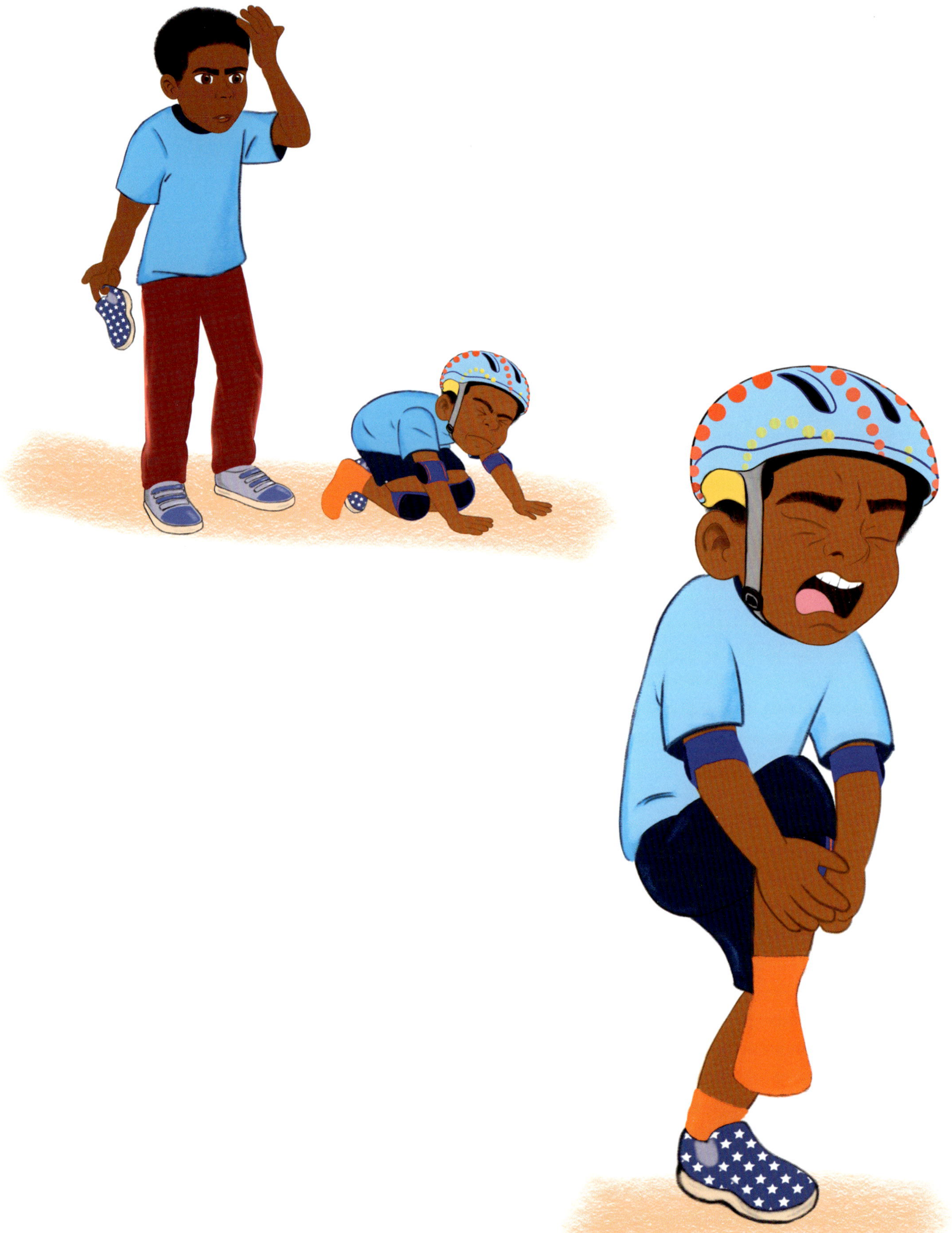

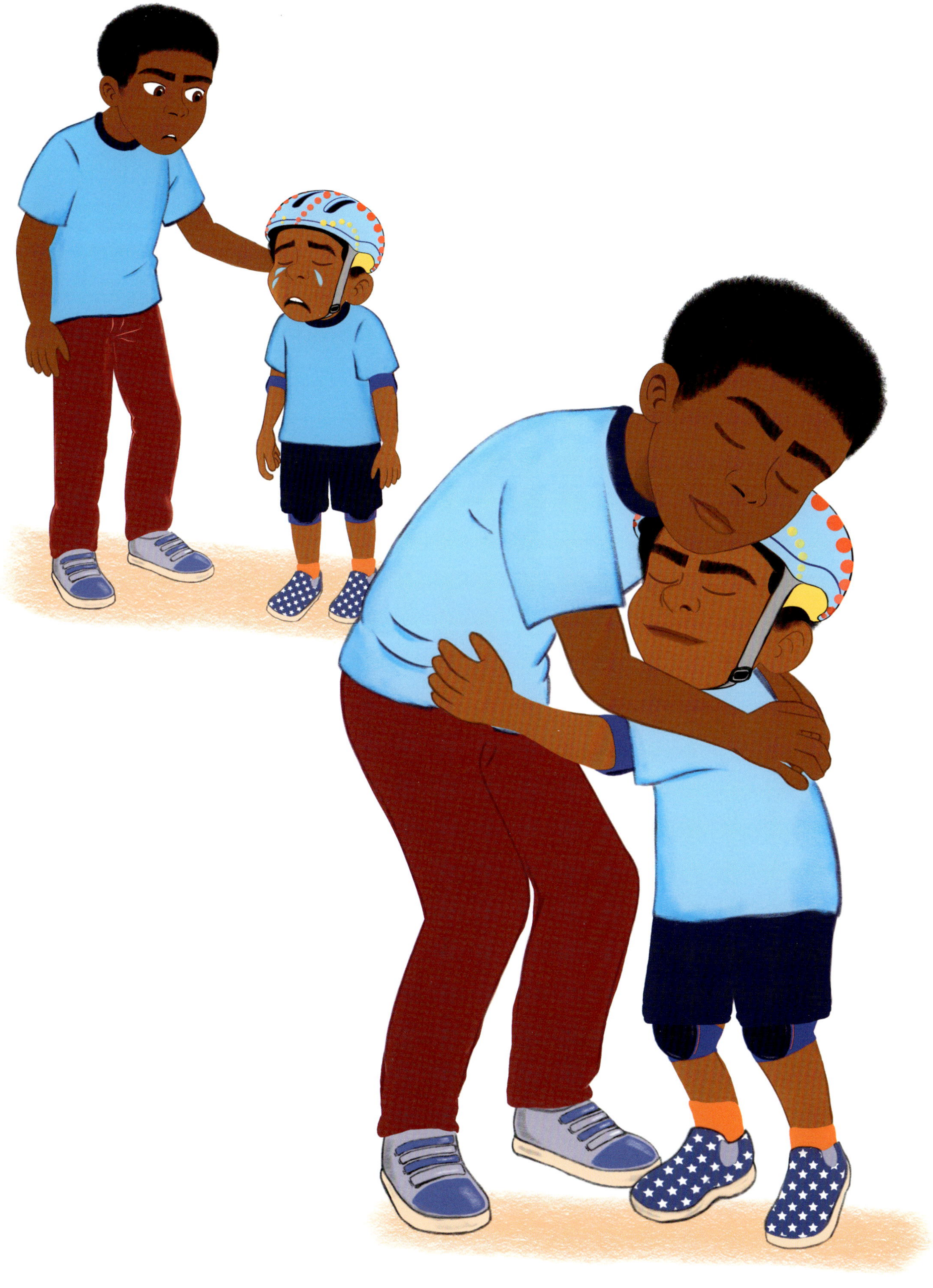

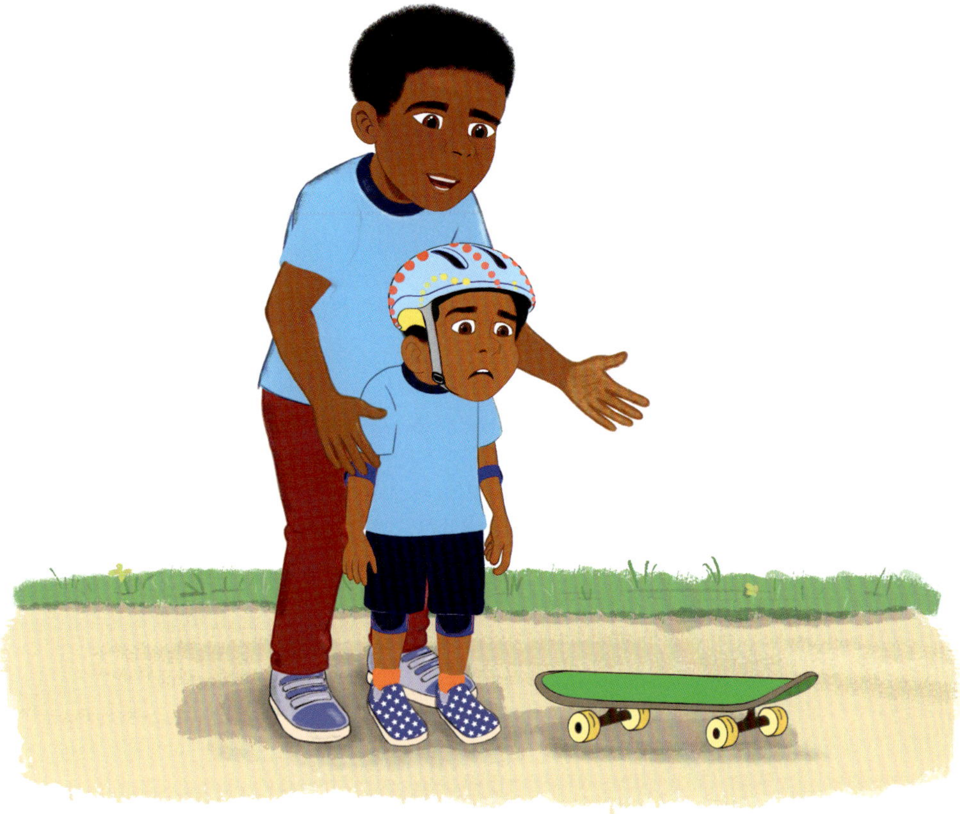

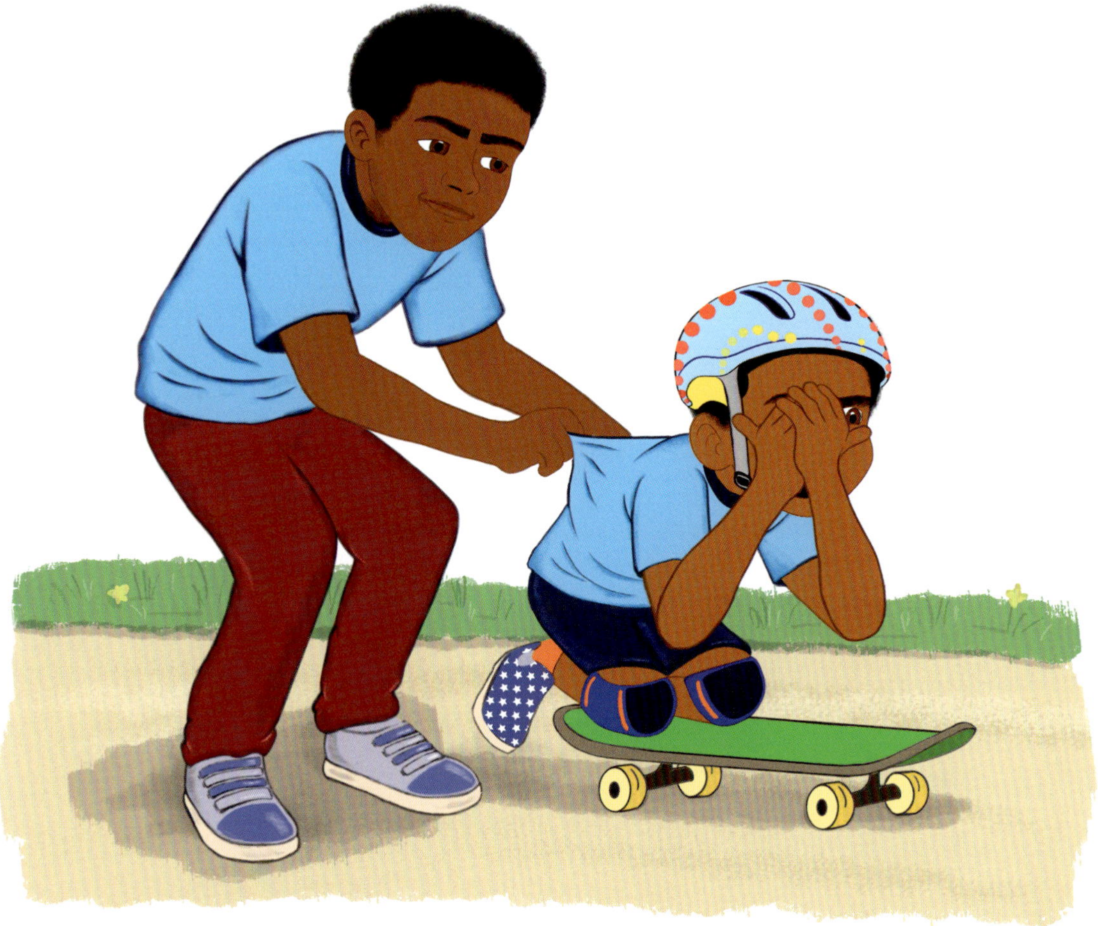

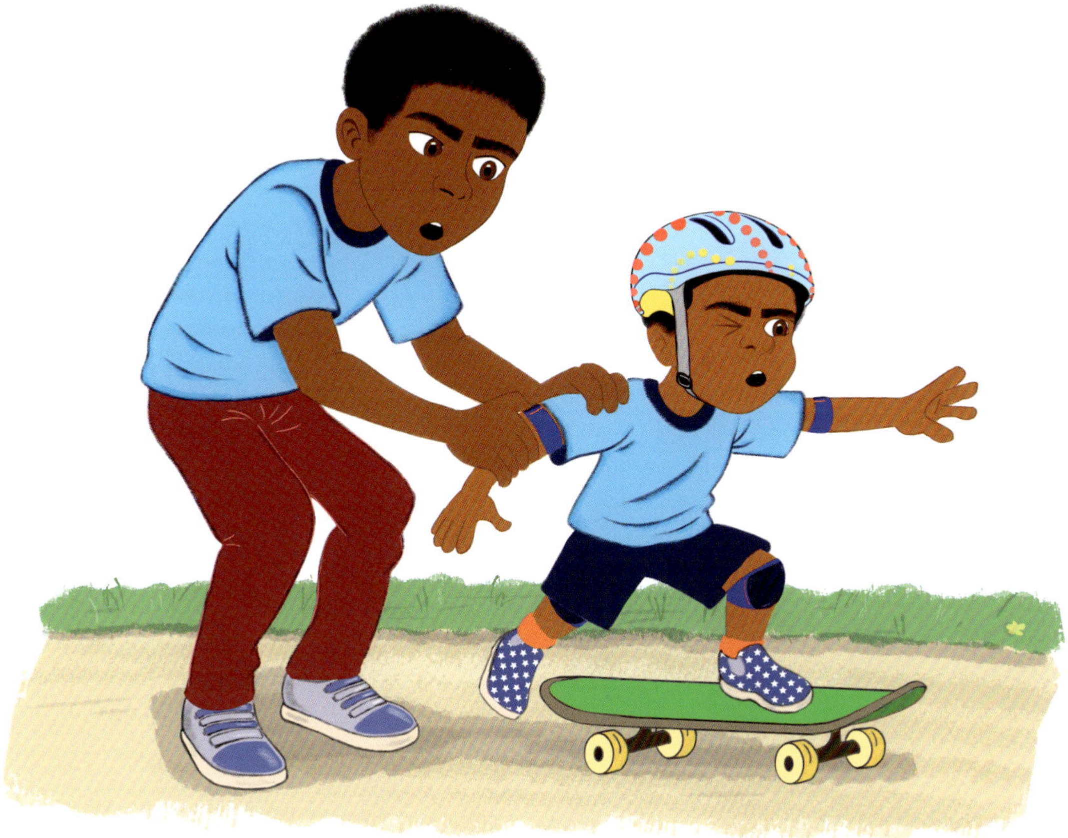

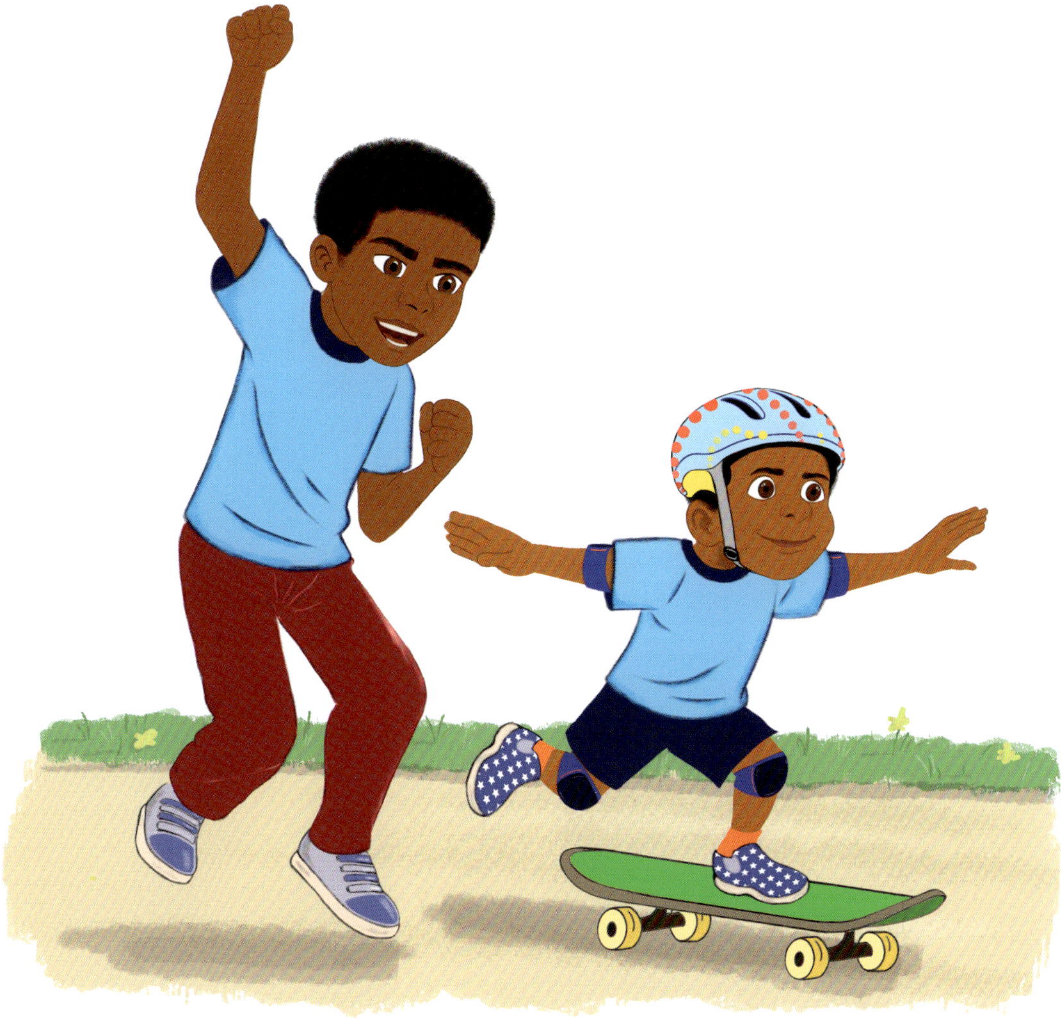

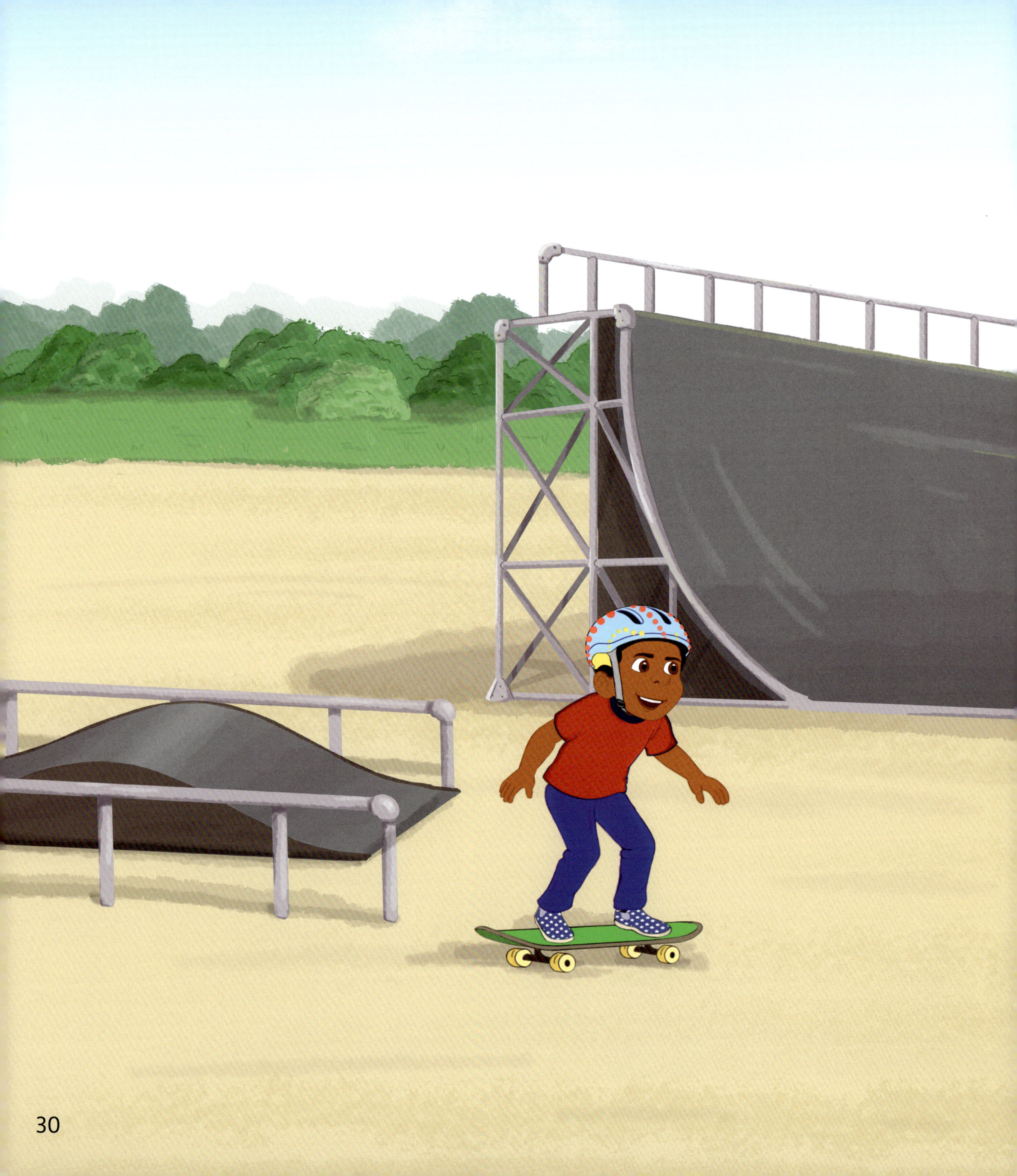

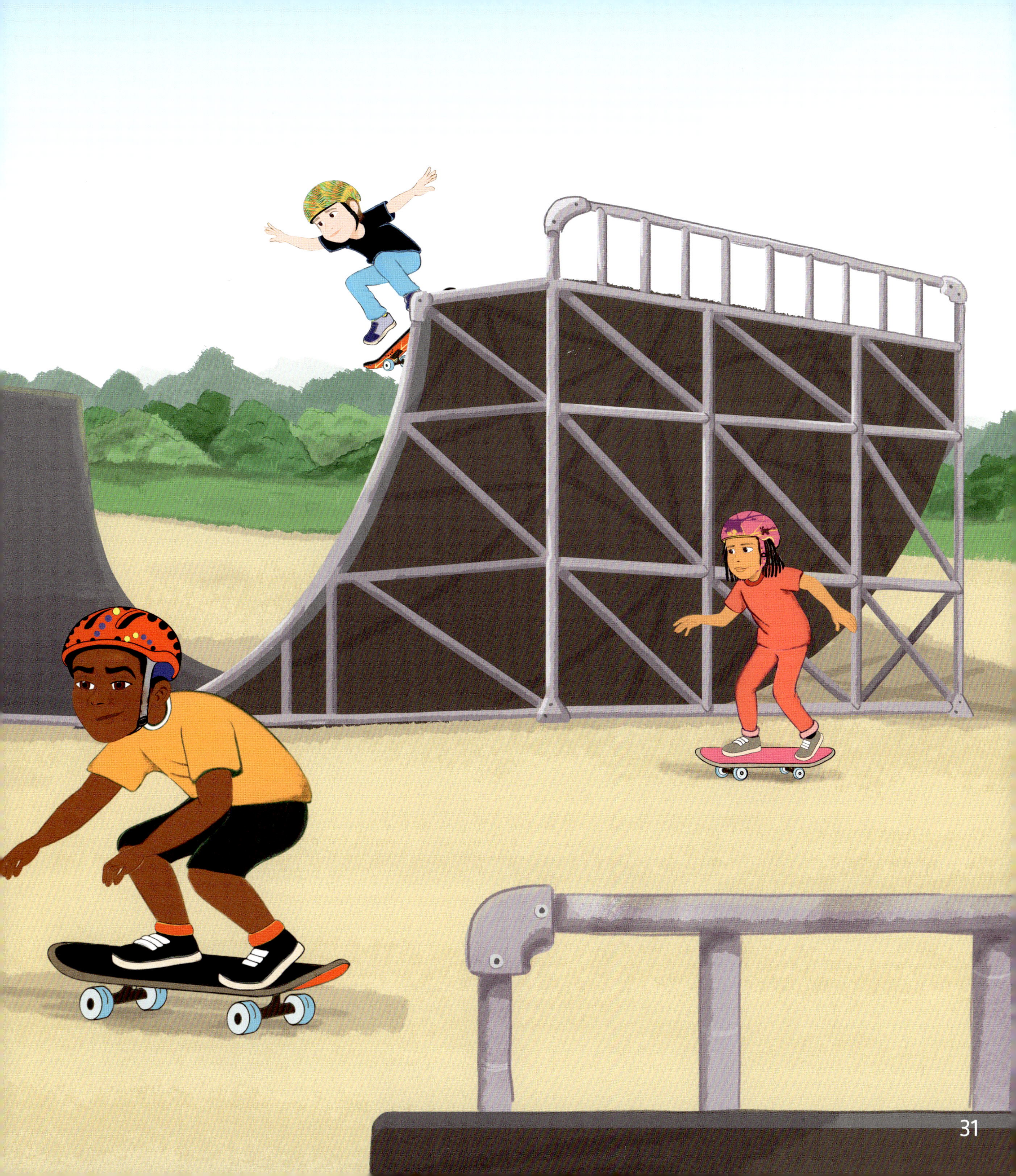

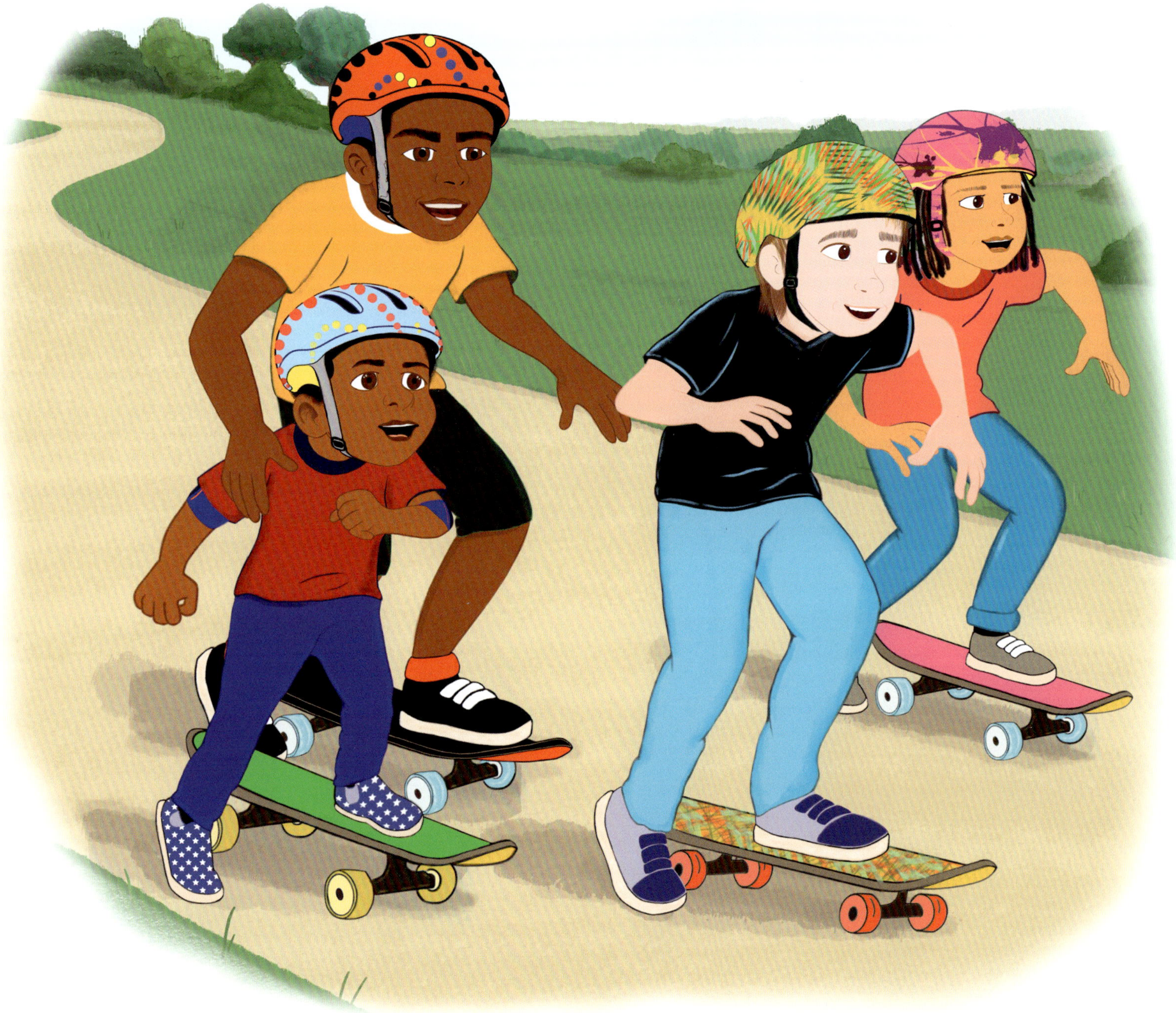